NAILED

RECLAIMING THE GOSPEL

JANET LOCK
SIMON MOUATT

RED BALLOON
PUBLISHING

A number of bible versions have been used when quoting scripture in this book:

Scripture quotations marked JB are from The Jerusalem Bible © 1966 by Darton, Longman & Todd Ltd and Doubleday and Company Ltd.

Scripture quotations marked Mounce are from the Mounce Reverse-Interlinear New Testament Copyright © 2011 by William D Mounce. Used by permission. All rights reserved worldwide.

Scripture quotations marked NASB are taken from the New American Standard Bible® (NASB), Copyright © 1960, 1962, 1963, 1968, 1971, 1972, 1973, 1975, 1977, 1995 by The Lockman Foundation Used by permission. www.Lockman.org

Scripture quotations marked NIV are taken from The Holy Bible, New International Version® NIV® Copyright © 1973 1978 1984 2011 by Biblica, Inc. ™ Used by permission. All rights reserved worldwide.

Scripture quotations marked NKJV are taken from the New King James Version®. Copyright © 1982 by Thomas Nelson. Used by permission. All rights reserved.

Scripture quotations marked NLT are taken from the Holy Bible, New Living Translation, copyright © 1996, 2004, 2015 by Tyndale House Foundation. Used by permission of Tyndale House Publishers, Inc., Carol Stream, Illinois 60188. All rights reserved.

Scripture quotations marked NRSV are from the New Revised

ABOUT THE AUTHORS

Simon Mouatt has believed in God as long as he can remember, and became a follower of Jesus in 1986. Since then he has been on a spiritual journey of discovery and growth, participating in a broad spectrum of church life. He has a passion for authentic theology and has given much time and thought to theological issues, his conclusions arising from biblical research, discourse with other believers, and seeking God. He has an interest in inter-faith and ecumenical dialogue, regularly participating in the Greenbelt festival, and speaking at inter-faith and political economy forums. Simon has an academic career spanning close to thirty years. He is author of two books on political economy and has contributed several chapters in published collaborative books and journals.

Janet Lock first believed in God as a child, and became a Christian in 1980. From the beginning of her spiritual journey she has had an interest in reconciliation, especially concerning brokenness and division in Europe. From 2001 to 2009 Janet and her husband lived in Germany, where she worked to promote trust and reconciliation. She was involved with intercessory activities and has instigated prayer initiatives in Germany and other nations. She helped establish a discipleship training course in Berlin where she was on the teaching team. She has had speaking engagements in several churches in Germany and Switzerland, as well as speaking at regional and church conferences.

FOREWORD

THE REVEREND PETER CHALLEN (FORMER CANON
SOUTHWARK CATHEDRAL)

The Christian faith is richly illuminated within the covers of this book, and will come into clearer focus by a careful reading of this diligently fashioned outline of the gospel. As followers of Christ, it encourages us to live as 'enthusiast' theologians, pursuing our daily round whilst applying our spiritual insights in every one of the challenges and opportunities each of us encounters.

This moving restatement of inclusive faith, in conjunction with the implications of incarnation—both Christ's and our own—is highly sensitive to each person's unique way of experiencing God in daily life. It contrasts the narrow sense of God being generously 'for us' with the boundless sense of God being intimately 'with us'.

The book is a biblically erudite, yet humble exploration into how God influences and flows within His mystic, eternal creativity—the reality we enjoy but do not control. Here, the gospel emerges again as good news, the truth that in our earthly life we are 'in Christ' and are able to discern His presence in all things. Absorbing this rich exploration of biblical relevance for our lives today may leave us deeply satisfied to be alive, whilst inseparably loving the sheer mystery we call God, and every representation of that mystery worked out amongst us.

Simply put, the book describes the double commandment with which we express our everyday eucharistic love, first assenting to God loving us, then loving Him and our neighbour in response. *Nailed* also offers us a bold rethinking of the primary concept of the priesthood of all believers, whereby we understand ourselves to be enthused servants of the living God in this vibrant universe of inclusivity, no longer defeated by the tyranny of 'original sin' but constantly refreshed by 'original blessing'.

ACKNOWLEDGMENTS

We are thankful to Catherine Mouatt and Bob Lock for their patience and support during the time of compiling this book. We have been encouraged by their thorough and intelligent consideration of all the subjects we have discussed here, and their diligence in correcting our grammar, and spotting our omissions. We also very much appreciate the comments and advice given by Tom Kurt, Steve Lancashire, Rebecca Lock, Steve Shepherd, Kate Pollard, Stephen Virgo, Rachel Searle and Peter Challen. Our book has benefited from their wisdom. The late Geoffrey Sansom and many other people, too numerous to mention, have influenced our understanding of God and the gospel, over many years.

CONTENTS

Nailed

Now Thomas (also known as Didymus), one of the Twelve, was not with the disciples when Jesus came. So the other disciples told him, 'We have seen the Lord!' But he said to them, 'Unless I see the nail marks in His hands and put my finger where the nails were, and put my hand into His side, I will not believe.' A week later His disciples were in the house again, and Thomas was with them. Though the doors were locked, Jesus came and stood among them and said, 'Peace be with you!' Then He said to Thomas, 'Put your finger here; see My hands. Reach out your hand and put it into My side. Stop doubting and believe.' (John 20:24-27 NIV).

BEGINNINGS

Jesus explained to His followers: 'Truly I tell you, unless you change and become like little children, you will never enter the kingdom of heaven' (Matthew 18:3 NIV). Jesus is not suggesting His followers become childish or irresponsible, nor that they discard their mental faculties. On the contrary, He is highlighting the fact that little children want to find things out, so they ask questions incessantly, without fear or shame, and they do not hold rigid opinions that would stop them wanting to play with other children who have different ideas. For small children the world is 'new every morning', each day bringing more things for them to discover. Likewise, Jesus is inviting us to approach His Father in simplicity, bringing Him all our questions, needs and fears. Even the eminent apostle Paul had this attitude, explaining to the Corinthian believers that despite his high level of education in Judaism he resolved to know nothing while he was with them, except Jesus Christ, and Him crucified. Paul thus came to them in weakness, and found his responsibility daunting (see 1 Corinthians 2:2-3). His resolve 'to know nothing' refers to his former academic religious learning. Yet Paul did know God, and he desired to know Him more. God redeemed Paul's intellect and entrusted him with explaining the message of Jesus to the gentile world.

The apostle Peter stated that all Christians are priests: 'You are a chosen race, a royal priesthood, a holy nation, a people for His own possession, so that you may declare (Greek: exangello) the goodness of Him who called you out of darkness into His marvellous light' (1 Peter 2:9). But Peter is also indicating here that the reason believers have this new, spiritual identity is so we can reveal to the world that our God is good. 'Exangello' means to make known, declare or publish. Whatever else believers may be called to do, displaying God's excellence in a world full of people who either discount Him altogether, or feel they cannot trust Him is probably the best thing we do. Christians are well-known for being outspoken on moral issues, and for their interpretation of biblical prophecy in respect of world politics. But concerning the mandate of making God's excellent nature known, it seems that the Church-at-large has all too often given an unappealing impression of God.

In recent years there has been a flurry of interest in

the Protestant Reformation of the 16th Century. Much of the theology that endures from the time of the Reformation was formulated by applying Greek logic to scripture. Subsequently those ideas were adopted as foundational to religious academic study, and have been used as a bedrock upon which others have built their theological ideas over the centuries. However, the Reformers had a sense of the times, and they had the courage to sweep away the religious assumptions of their day. In our view it is appropriate to take a fresh look at scripture for our own times, not assuming it necessary to refer back to Reformation theology, but instead going direct to source scripture. Today there are many wonderful bible resources readily available online, in particular Greek interlinear texts, that afford all believers a new opportunity to discover the original intention of the writers of the New Testament. Certainly Jesus wanted everyone to understand His message, without any need for academic interpretation. His message was of a loving God who makes Himself available to everyone. Any theology that could alienate people from God must be thoroughly revised.

In this book we have outlined our understanding of the Trinity, with the intention of showing God's goodness and kindness, and we have presented our view of how the Trinity relates to humanity. We have set out our ideas in a number of statements, in the manner of Martin Luther, who publicly nailed 95 theses to a church door, an act which eventually led to the

Protestant Reformation. Through our ideas we hope to challenge readers to engage their thinking, to re-examine source biblical texts and to check whether the ideas they have heard are in alignment with the nature of God, as revealed by Jesus. We also encourage readers to bring their thoughts, opinions and theology to God in prayer, and to ask what His opinions are. The bible encourages believers to 'be transformed by the renewing of your mind' (Romans 12:2), which suggests this is probably God's principal way of conforming believers to the character of Christ. As we humble ourselves before God, acknowledging that we need to learn more from Him until our last breath, He will reveal His ways to us. It is the unshakable knowledge that God is always trustworthy, kind and good, that provides an anchor for the human soul.

We have formed our view of Christianity, as expressed here, over several decades. Whilst remaining truth seekers, we are comfortable with our present understanding of God, and hope that others may benefit from reading this. Although our book is entitled 'Nailed', no-one has a monopoly on the truth, and this book must certainly be considered with that in mind, but it does, in the words of our friend Canon Peter Challen, represent an honest yet tentative conviction at the time of writing.

INTRODUCTION

This book has twelve chapters, divided into three sections relating to Jesus Christ, the Holy Spirit and Father God, which we have associated with the concepts of faith, hope and love, respectively. Every chapter has eight statements, each with its own narrative explanation. Please give yourself time to think and pray about each narrative rather than reading all at once.

We have called followers of Christ 'believers' rather than 'Christians'—a term that only occurs three times in the entire New Testament. Before reading, please bear in mind our presuppositions, as set out below:

First, the principles we set ourselves when writing this book were that it would be concise, inclusive, and verifiable by the reader. We recommend, in particular, that you use online resources which give access to the original Greek of the New Testament.

Second, it is our contention that the scriptures have too often been used by some for ambitious purpose, against the best interests of people and the earth. Since there are many wording options when translating source Greek and Aramaic texts into English, translators' work has often been influenced by assumptions based on their worldview and theological positions. We have used the Mounce Reverse-Interlinear New Testament for many scripture references, acknowledging the contribution this has made to scholarly bible study for all. When quoting a passage of scripture we have given the bible reference and version, unless we have used our own paraphrase.

For purposes of clarity we have capitalised pronouns that appertain to Deity.

Third, the book is not intended to tell you, the reader, how to think, but to prompt you to give fresh consideration to the New Testament, and in particular, the gospels. We invite you to enter into dialogue with us and other believers, not to arrive at rigid theological ideas, but to give scope to the Holy Spirit to continue developing your understanding of God and His ways. We contend that God is pleased to give each believer the relevant wisdom when they seek it.

Fourth, Jesus made God accessible by living with humanity, and He made His teachings accessible by using simple words. Although His parables were mysteries, He would give explanations to anyone who wanted to understand. He welcomes us when we come to Him asking for clarification. We recommend that this attitude of seeking should pervade the believers' whole approach to spiritual matters.

Fifth, we assert that the Trinity does all things in consonance and cannot be divided. At the same time, mysteriously, there are three Persons—the Father, Son and Holy Spirit. The Trinity is united in the process of creation, salvation, sanctification and judgment. In this sense, we are formed by all three Persons. God is love, and love needs to flow to be love, in the same way that electricity needs to flow to be electricity. Thus love flows between the Persons of the Trinity. Since love existed before the beginning of time, God has always been the Trinity—if God were merely one person He would have had to love Himself. But in fact, His love and regard are unselfish, outward-flowing and sacrificial, honouring the other before Himself—
    kindness rather than self-indulgence,
    giving rather than taking,
    forgiving rather than punishing,
    empowering rather than controlling,
    submitting rather than hurting,
    encouraging rather than winning.

In short, we assert that God's character is beautiful.

FAITH: ENTRY INTO THE KINGDOM

A WORK OF JESUS CHRIST

1

THE NATURE OF THE GOSPEL

1. The gospel is good news
2. The gospel does not contain any guile
3. The gospel is not a philosophy or ideology
4. The gospel is not a code of behaviour
5. The gospel is not grasped through human reason
6. The gospel is only received by revelation
7. The gospel pertains to everything
8. The gospel is for the benefit of everyone

---

1 ¶ THE GOSPEL IS GOOD NEWS

The word 'gospel' means a message of good news. The first four books of the New Testament are commonly called the gospels precisely because they convey to the reader a message that is potentially life-transforming. The message that Christ preached was that 'the Kingdom of God is at hand'. And through His teachings, through the things He did and the way He interacted with people, He revealed the true nature of the Kingdom of God. The good news is that the unseen realm of God, which provides love and security for those who believe, is available as an alternative to the uncertainty of self-reliance, and the buffeting of random human behaviours: 'He has rescued us from the tyranny of darkness and transferred us into the kingdom of His beloved Son, in whom we have redemption, the forgiveness of sins' (Colossians 1:13-14 Mounce). The apostle Paul defined the gospel as 'the power of God for salvation to everyone who believes' (Romans 1:16). When people are impacted by the gospel for the first time, they are amazed that they begin to experience an entirely new dimension of life, which is immediately available to them. However, if the message given is not perceived as good news it is either not the gospel, or those who hear have no sense of their need. Thus the message of Christ actually brings good news to the afflicted—people who sense something in life is missing —by offering the solution that will satisfy: As Jesus said, 'I am the bread of life; the one who comes to me will never go hungry, and the one who believes in me will never be thirsty again' (John 6:35).

Since the fall of humankind, people have had all kinds of false ideas about what their creator God is like. Even the religious people of Jesus' day misunderstood Him, despite the law they were rigorously following. But as people heard the gospel message and believed it, they would reconnect with God: 'Through Christ, God was reconciling the world to Himself, not counting their trespasses against them. And He has entrusted us with the message of reconciliation. Therefore we are ambassadors for Christ, as though God makes His appeal through us, we implore you on behalf of Christ, "Be reconciled to God"' (2 Corinthians 5:18-20). It is important that God literally came in person to rescue us, because Christ displays the true, vulnerable nature of God, and the magnitude of God's love for all people. Wherever He went Jesus announced that the Kingdom of God is now within reach: 'Early in the morning Jesus went out to an isolated place. The crowds searched everywhere for Him, and when they finally found Him, they begged Him not to leave them. But He replied, "I must preach the Good News of the Kingdom of God in other towns too, because this is why I was sent"' (Luke 4:42-43). Jesus also embodied the long awaited promise which God made on the day Adam and Eve were deceived: Jesus, born of a woman, was the 'Seed' that was to crush Satan's head (see Genesis 3:15). Thus the gospel is the good news that humanity has always been waiting for, and ultimately it promises to be even better than we could possibly imagine, as it is written: 'eye has not seen, nor ear heard, nor have entered into the human heart the things which God has prepared for those who love Him' (1 Corinthians 2:9).

---

2 ¶ THE GOSPEL DOES NOT CONTAIN ANY GUILE

Jesus does not sugarcoat His message in order to gain new recruits. On the contrary, He warns people that there is personal cost involved in following Him, and inevitable troubles. He gives no promise of utopia on this earth, and no immunity from the sufferings of life. Jesus warned people to think seriously before deciding to follow Him: 'Whoever does not carry his own cross and come after Me cannot be My disciple. If anyone wants to build a tower, he first calculates the cost to see whether he has enough money to finish it; otherwise, if he lays the foundations but cannot complete the tower, everyone will laugh at him. Or if a king who has ten thousand troops is about to go to war against another king who has twenty thousand, he will consider whether he has a chance of winning. If not, he will send a delegation to ask for terms of peace' (see Luke 14:27-32). In both Jesus' examples, hasty decisions made in a moment of enthusiasm could end in humiliation or disaster. Jesus also explained that if we belong to His Kingdom we are likely to be despised, rejected, even victimised: 'If you belonged to the world, the world would love you as its own, but you do not belong to the world. Since I chose you out of the world, the world hates you. Remember I told you, "The servant is not greater than his master." If they persecuted Me they will persecute you too; if they kept My word they will keep yours too. Whatever they do to you will be on account of My name, because they do not know the One who sent Me' (see John 15:19-21). This does not sound like good news, but that depends on where our treasure is. Once we have encountered Christ as the one who satisfies our spiritual longing, we realise that our earthly life is a shadow compared to eternity: 'Our outward person is wasting away, yet our inward person is being renewed day by day. The momentary light affliction we suffer is producing an eternal weight of glory for us, way beyond all comparison. So we do not focus on what can be seen, but on what is unseen, because what can be seen is transitory, but what is unseen is eternal' (2 Corinthians 4:16-18).

As believers we can experience fulfilment in this life and we know we are loved, but even our suffering works in our favour. We have not been tricked.

---

3 ¶ THE GOSPEL IS NOT A PHILOSOPHY OR AN IDEOLOGY

The Oxford dictionary describes a philosophy as a belief, theory or attitude that may act as a guiding principle for behaviour, whereas an ideology is a system of ideas and ideals held by an individual or a group which directly determines their actions, in the same manner as a religion. In 313 A.D. the Emperor Constantine chose to adopt Christianity as the religion of his empire. The theoretical principles of Christianity provided him with great benefits for keeping law and order, and soliciting respectful behaviour in society. The guiding principle usually taken from Jesus' teaching is: 'Do unto others as you would have others do unto you' (Luke 6:31). When people abide by this one rule alone, life becomes better for everyone, including the rulers. People sometimes say 'Britain is no longer a Christian country', but in fact they are alluding to the demise of philosophical values derived from Christianity. However, the gospel is not a philosophy, it is an introduction to the person of Jesus Christ, with whom we are encouraged to have a real friendship. The gospel is thus not a system of ideas to be imposed. When an individual becomes a believer, a transformation process begins, which continues until the end of life. The Holy Spirit convicts them of the things God wishes to change in their lives, and as they allow Him to renew their minds, their attitudes and understanding will progressively conform to His. But it is unreasonable to require others to conform to the ideals which believers contend are right and godly. A person who has received revelation about a particular issue cannot then impose their standard on anyone else—whether believers or non-believers—nor do they have the right to condemn others. The apostle Paul writes: 'What business is it of mine to judge outsiders?' (1 Corinthians 5:12). Non-believers may view Christians as bigots and hypocrites when they attempt to apply their values to society. However, when led by God, believers will speak up for the oppressed, the poor, the victims of injustice, and against the spoiling of the earth's environment. In that case, the motivator is not philosophy or ideology, but their relationship with Christ.

---

4 ¶ The gospel is not a code of behaviour

Unlike the gospel, the Old Testament Law was a code of behaviour, designed to keep God's covenanted people on the right path. People feel safe when they have a rule-book, clear instructions and somebody to tell them what to do and think. The demands of the Law were stringent, but people were able to comply with its requirements if they made enough effort. In His sermon on the mount, Jesus told His listeners that these rules were insufficient for pleasing God—and He set new standards that were impossible to attain through human effort. The crowd must have been shocked (see Matthew 5:20-49). He was introducing the concept that only by grace are people able to live in a way that pleases God, thus enabling us to rest from obligation to fulfil the Law by self-effort. The new covenant operates through this grace, whereby the believer receives the supernatural resources to accomplish the things that God prepared beforehand for him or her to do. The law of Christ is written in the hearts and minds of believers (see Jeremiah 31:33) and they overcome the obligation to focus on the demands of religious law by completely ignoring it, in favour of a trusting relationship with the Lord. Believers do not need the law to inform them of the correct or wrong behaviour since they know when they have fallen short, and falling short is a regular occurrence for most people. At these times, believers know that God forgives them, and they then carry on their journey with the assurance that His unconditional love will cause them to grow in grace, and the knowledge of Christ.

Although succeeded by a far better covenant arrangement (see Hebrews 8:6), even the earlier Mosaic Law was originally given to the Israelites by God through love. However, Jesus criticised the religious leaders for mis-interpreting the Law of Moses and, over time, adding their own burdensome rules to it: 'Some Pharisees and scribes from Jerusalem asked Jesus, "Why do Your disciples break the tradition of the elders? They do not wash their hands when they eat bread." Jesus replied, "Why do you ignore the commandment of God for the sake of your tradition? For God said, 'Honour your father and mother,' and, 'He who speaks evil of father or mother is to be put to death.' But you say, 'If someone tells his father or mother, "Whatever help I could have given you has been dedicated to God," he need not honour his father or mother.' Thus you have annulled the word of God for the sake of your tradition.

You are hypocrites, and Isaiah prophesied about you: 'This people honours Me with their lips, but their hearts are far from Me. They worship Me in vain, teaching the human rules as doctrines'" (Matthew 15:1-9). The religious leaders of Jesus' day were guardians of their own religious rulebook, but had missed the heart of God in the Law of Moses, as summed up by Christ: 'You shall love the Lord your God with all your heart, and with all your soul, and with all your mind. This is the great and foremost commandment. The second is like it, you shall love your neighbour as yourself. The entire Law and the Prophets hang on these two commandments' (Matthew 22:37-40). In the new covenant, people please God by believing in Christ rather than by fulfilling the Law, as Jesus explained to the crowd, 'This is the work that God requires, that you believe in Him whom He has sent' (John 6:29).

---

5 ¶ THE GOSPEL IS NOT GRASPED THROUGH HUMAN REASON

The meaning of the gospel message is not intended to make sense solely by human wisdom: 'In His wisdom, God arranged it that the world did not come to know Him through its wisdom. But God is pleased to save people who believe through the foolishness of what we preach. Jews demand miraculous proof and Greeks want logical reasoning, but we preach Christ crucified, which is offensive to Jews and illogical to Gentiles, but for those called, Christ is the power of God and the wisdom of God. So, God's foolishness is wiser than the wisdom of men, and God's weakness is stronger than the strength of men' (1 Corinthians 1:21-25). Today, Christian theology can be studied as an academic subject by anyone who is interested. But when a person's knowledge about God is received in the same way as a history lesson, it has no effect beyond providing information. Thus, the power to transform a human life is absent until God gives revelation.

As God continues to give believers an unfolding of the scope and implications of the gospel, this also requires divine wisdom, and not human reason. The apostle Paul was careful to point out to the Corinthians, who had a propensity to elevate their teachers as heroes, that his own cleverness was irrelevant: 'I did not use superior speech or wisdom when I explained the mystery of God to you. I made the decision to know nothing, except Jesus Christ, and Him crucified. I remained in weakness, in fear and trembling, and you were not persuaded by any eloquence or cleverness of mine, but by a demonstration of the Spirit and of power. So your faith is not based on the wisdom of men, but on the power of God' (see 1 Corinthians 2:1-5). In this passage Paul is indicating that God does not intend Christian teachers to rely on the knowledge they have accumulated, but that they allow the Holy Spirit to give them words pertinent to the listeners. Whilst, for a variety of reasons, our intellectual rumination can be beneficial, the life transforming gospel is initially perceived in the human spirit, revealed to the human mind, and thereafter the mind continues to process it.

---

6 ¶ THE GOSPEL IS ONLY RECEIVED BY REVELATION

Paul wrote: 'I want you to know, brothers and sisters, that the gospel I preached is not of human origin. I did not receive it from any man, nor was I taught it; rather I received it by revelation from Jesus Christ' (Galatians 1:11-12 NIV). Since the revelation of the gospel is initiated in the heavenly realms, and is recognised as such by those who receive it through grace, this means it is not a man-made creation of the mind. Jesus describes this aspect of the gospel thus: 'All things have been handed over to me by My Father and no one knows who the Son is except the Father, or who the Father is except the Son and anyone to whom the Son decides to reveal Him' (Luke 10:22 Mounce). When Jesus asked His disciples, 'Who do you say that I am?', Simon Peter replied, 'You are the Christ, the Son of the living God'. Jesus responded, saying to Peter, 'You are blessed Simon son of Jonah because flesh and blood did not reveal this to you, but My Father in heaven'. Afterwards Jesus ordered His disciples to tell nobody that He was the Christ (see Matthew 16:13-17 & 20). In the gospel accounts we can observe that Jesus does not proclaim His identity, but rather He gives people space to receive personal revelation from the Father about who He is. However, when people had received revelation about His identity, Jesus was pleased to confirm it. For example, the woman with whom Jesus had a conversation at Jacob's well, said, 'I know that Messiah is coming (the one called Christ). When He comes, He will explain everything to us.' Jesus said to her, 'I, the one speaking to you, am He' (John 4:25-26 Mounce). The religious leaders, however, had made up their minds that Jesus was an impostor, as we see in the account of the blind young man whom Jesus healed. When questioned by the Pharisees, his parents were unwilling to acknowledge this miracle because they were afraid of the Jewish leaders, who had already decided that anyone who acknowledged Jesus was the Messiah, would be put out of the synagogue (see John 9:22). The Pharisees were seeking a confrontation with Jesus when they asked, 'How long will You keep us in suspense? If You are the Christ, tell us plainly.' Jesus replied, 'I told you, and you do not believe; the works that I do in My Father's name, these testify of Me' (John 10:24-25). Jesus was unwilling to persuade them by means of human argument.

People may believe they themselves set out to find God, but in fact He seeks after them, and He Himself initiates the human desire for Himself. Then, as people respond to Him He gives them a revelation of His reality, which marks the start of their relationship with

Him. Thereafter, He gives continuing revelation to His children because He wants them to know His ways.

---

7 ¶ THE GOSPEL PERTAINS TO EVERYTHING

The New Testament makes it clear that all things were made through Christ, and all things are sustained by Him: 'For by Him all things were created, both in the heavens and on earth, visible and invisible, whether thrones or dominions or rulers or authorities—all things have been created through Him and for Him. He is before all things, and in Him all things hold together' (Colossians 1:16-17 NASB). And yet, motivated by love for us, He chose to be made man, to live with us, to explain accurately the ways of God, and purposefully to die a bloody death, before rising again. The gospel message tells us that the kingdom of heaven has been made easily accessible to all people, simply through believing in Christ.

According to theologians, John wrote his gospel in about 85 A.D. and despite all the passing years since the ascension, he was still filled with wonder that he actually spent time with Christ, the God of all things: 'In the beginning was the Word, and the Word was with God, and the Word was God. He was in the beginning with God. All things came into being through Him, and apart from Him nothing came into being that has come into being' (John 1:1-3 NASB). John furthermore explains that Christ entered into His own creation in order to retrieve that which was stolen from Him: 'The true Light which enlightens everyone came into the world. He was in the world, the world that was created by Him, yet the world did not know Him. He came to the people He had embraced as His own, yet His own people did not embrace Him. But to those who did accept Him He gave the right to become children of God, to the ones who believe in His name, born not of natural descent nor fleshly choice nor a husband's decision, but of God' (John 1:9-13).

Believers have Christ dwelling within them, as their king. And He exercises His reign from within. On one occasion the Pharisees asked Jesus when the Kingdom of God would come. He explained that, 'The Kingdom of God will not come with observable signs; nor will anyone say, "Look over here!" or "Look over there!" Because the Kingdom of God is within you' (Luke 17:20-21). Thus the Kingdom of God can reign in every aspect of a believer's life, and their realm of influence.

8 ¶ THE GOSPEL IS FOR THE BENEFIT OF EVERYONE

Jesus said to the disciples: 'Go into all the world and proclaim the gospel to every creature' (Mark 16:15 Mounce). No-one is excluded from becoming a disciple of Christ, which means having direct access to an intimate relationship with God, learning from Him, and discovering His purpose for one's life: 'God loved the world so much that He gave His one and only Son, that everyone who believes in Him will not perish but have eternal life. God did not sent His Son into the world to judge the world, but to save the world through Him' (John 3:16-17). The death and resurrection of Christ expresses the love of the Father for humanity: 'God puts His own love for us on public display, in that while we were still sinners Christ died for us' (Romans 5:8).

Scripture suggests that even the promise of Christ's return has been delayed in order to give everyone an opportunity to receive salvation: 'The Lord is not late in fulfilling His promise, as some measure lateness, but is patient, not wanting anyone to perish, but that all would come to repentance' (2 Peter 3:9). People might reasonably ask, since God is omnipresent, as Christian theology claims, why are people not aware of Him all the time? God is Spirit, and it is only the human spirit which is able to commune at a spiritual level. But since the fall of Adam and Eve, the human spirit is enclosed within the human soul. When the soul is self-satisfied a person may not see any need for God. But when people sense something is wrong or missing in their life they are more likely to respond to Him. As Jesus explained: 'It is not those who are well who need a physician, but those who are sick. I have not come to call the righteous but sinners to repentance' (Luke 5:31-32 NASB). Many people are living with sickness in their body that they are unaware of, and they will not go to the doctor until they have symptoms that bother them. The fragile human condition means that eventually all will realise they need a doctor. In a similar way, the ultimate failure of the soul to satisfy spiritual longings can prompt us to seek God. Since all humans share these common weaknesses, it is encouraging to know that the gospel is intended for everyone.

2

THE WORK OF CHRIST

9. Christ came to destroy the works of Satan
10. Christ became the Son of Man
11. Christ reintroduces us to His Father
12. Christ willingly gave His life for us
13. Christ took the consequences of our sin
14. Christ removes our sense of condemnation
15. Christ has been given the authority to judge
16. Christ gives us eternal life

9 ¶ CHRIST CAME TO DESTROY THE WORKS OF SATAN

The incarnation of Christ was for the specific task of overcoming the world system that Satan set up to hold human beings captive to his will: 'The reason the Son of God appeared was to destroy the works of the devil' (1 John 3:8). The devil is real, and as Jesus explained, his only purpose is to 'steal and kill and destroy' (John 10:10). He seeks to steal our peace, joy and sense of destiny, and to destroy our relationship with God. Yet believers are empowered to overcome these attacks, by faith, because of Christ's finished work on the cross.

During His earthly ministry, Jesus went around doing good and healing all who were oppressed by the devil. However, Satan continues to influence the powers and structures of this world, which causes much suffering. Nevertheless, through Jesus, it is possible for anybody to have access to the God of love. Thereafter, once people have an intimate relationship with Him, even the devil and all his schemes cannot come between them and God. As Paul wrote, 'I am convinced that neither death nor life, neither angels nor demons, neither the present nor the future, nor any powers, neither height nor depth, nor anything else in all creation, will be able to separate us from the love of God that is in Christ Jesus our Lord' (Romans 8:38-39 NIV).

However, the devil remains the ruler of this world (see John 14:30) through his web of deceit, and since believers are living in the world, he will continue to try and cause us to stumble with the aim of destroying our faith. The most common way he does this is through lying to us, the same trick he used on Adam and Eve. As Peter explained: 'Your enemy, the devil, walks around like a roaring lion looking for someone to devour, therefore be on your guard and resist him' (1 Peter 5:8-9). Jesus made this very clear during a discourse with some religious Jews, 'the devil was a murderer from the beginning and is an enemy of truth because there is no truth in him. When he speaks a lie he is expressing his own nature, because he is a liar, and the father of lies' (John 8:44). The thoughts that enter our minds are not necessarily generated by us, they can come from anywhere; from something we have heard, from memories, as well as the lies and evil suggestions coming from the devil. Therefore, when we get a negative thought, this is not a sin but we are advised to take every thought captive to the obedience of Christ in order to prevent it affecting our heart.

Satan also seeks to kill our bodies. But although believers are mortal and therefore vulnerable, Christ's death and resurrection has the power to free us from intimidation by the threat of death. 'Christ shared our human state of flesh and blood, so that through His death He could disempower the devil, who holds the power of death, and free people who were in bondage throughout their life through the fear of death' (see Hebrews 2:14-15). Jesus raised several people from the dead during His earthly ministry, demonstrating that He had power over death. However, these people still experienced death at some point in the future, because of sin: 'If Christ is in you, although the body is dead because of sin, the spirit is alive because of righteousness' (Romans 8:10). When Jesus rose again after the crucifixion He was given a resurrection body, which is different from the natural human body, and was evidence of His overcoming the world. The resurrection body of Christ is not subject to death, as Romans 6:9 explains: 'Since Christ has been raised from the dead, never to die again, death no longer has any power over Him'. Believers will also be raised with Him: 'With the resurrection of the dead, the body sown is perishable, it is raised imperishable; it is sown in dishonour, it is raised in glory' (1 Corinthians 15:42-43). Christ defeated the works of Satan, including the power of death. Believers can also have assurance that in the age to come, Satan will finally be rendered powerless (see Revelation 20:10).

10 ¶ Christ became the Son of Man

From eternity, Jesus Christ was part of the Trinitarian Godhead—God the Son. Yet, His call was to relinquish the heavenly glory that was His, in order to be born a helpless human baby. He took this drastic step with a very specific objective. Christ was born of a woman and thus He became an authentic representative of humankind. But at the same time He retained His divinity. The traditional catechism of the church used by Christians for centuries, describes this dual identity succinctly: 'The incarnation of the Son of God does not mean that Jesus Christ is part God and part man, nor does it imply that He is the result of a confused mixture of the divine and the human. He became truly man while remaining truly God. Jesus Christ is true God and true man.'

In the gospel accounts Jesus often refers to Himself as the Son of Man. The Greek word here translated as 'man', is 'anthropos', which literally means 'humanity'. Since His incarnation, Christ has become a representative for all humanity. And just as Adam, the forefather of the whole human race, was a representative of all who were 'in his loins' (see Hebrews 7:9-10) when he complied with the devil's suggestion, all have been subjected to the devil's deception and influence ever since. Jesus Christ was born as a new representative for humanity, another Adam, because He was born uncontaminated by the effects of the fall. This was to provide humankind with a second chance.

Mary, Jesus' mother, was a virgin who was engaged to Joseph, and she had not yet had sexual relations with a man. But the conception of Jesus was instigated by the Holy Spirit, as He overshadowed Mary. So, although the gospel of Matthew records the genetic line of Joseph, Jesus does not have a genetic inheritance from Joseph. Conversely, from a racial standpoint, a baby is designated Jewish if born to a Jewish mother. Therefore Jesus was born a Jew, born under the Law of Moses; and born into the covenant God made with Abram, which was founded on God making promises, and Abram believing them. Whilst we know that in Christ there is no male or female (see Galatians 3:28), the genealogies of Jesus in the gospels portray the inheritance of Adam through the male blood line (see Luke 3:23-38). In order to explain why Jesus was uncontaminated by the fall, it is sometimes taught that Mary was sinless. We contend however, that sin is common to all human beings. Yet, just as some genetic defects are transmitted through the bloodline of one gender, and not the other, perhaps the inheritance of the fall is transmitted through the male line, as implied in the Law of Moses. This would explain why Jesus, although fully human, was not born subjected to the deception of the fall.

At the beginning of His ministry Jesus was exposed to temptations similar to those experienced by Adam and Eve. The Holy Spirit led Jesus into the wilderness where He fasted for forty days. When He had become desperately hungry, the devil tried to tempt Him to eat. But Christ resisted, speaking words from scripture as a counter measure. He used scripture because that was the resource given by God to human beings. Jesus did not use any means other than what was available to every Jewish person. The devil then tried to tempt Jesus further, to entice Him to act independently of His Father. Again Jesus resisted, quoting scripture to contradict satan's propositions. Thereby Christ did what Adam failed to do.

Even though Jesus overcame this intense onslaught, He continued to be bombarded with spiritual attacks throughout His time on earth. But He kept faithful to His task and prayed for the resources of heaven to help. Jesus was not given any shortcuts or privileges that were specific to Him, because when dealing with the devil's assaults He was representing the human race, and His choices had to come exclusively from His own humanity. During Jesus' lifetime He lived a blameless human life, living in daily relationship and dependancy on God, as Adam originally did. His teachings were designed to explain to people how God's kingdom functions, and to expose the deceptions of religion. His acceptance of all people as of equal value demonstrates God's intention of the way human beings are meant to treat one another. Christ's life was exemplary, giving a perfect model for a godly human life. He is the paradigm for all believers, always expressing kindness, wisdom, compassion and humility, demonstrating our spiritual union with God and with each other.

When Jesus was taken by the Roman soldiers and nailed to the cross, He was representative of all humanity who believe in Him thus, in a very real sense, 'we have been crucified with Christ' (see Galatians 2:19-20). We are also, in a mystical sense, 'seated with Him in heavenly places', since, to borrow the language of the writers of Hebrews, we were in Christ's loins when He died. Just as all the children of Israel who were yet to be born were in Abraham's loins when he gave tithes to Melchizedek (see Hebrews 7:9-10). In the case of Jesus, believers are, of course, spiritual descendants, but importantly, so are all those who are yet to be reborn. Jesus prayed on behalf of these in His high priestly prayer: 'Father, I also pray for all those who will come to believe in Me through their word (John 17:20).

After Jesus was crucified on our behalf and rose again, He appeared in the midst of His disciples, and showed Thomas His wrists, which bore the nail marks from His crucifixion. This means that Christ's resurrection body still carries the marks of His crucifixion. He recurrently appeared to His followers over a period of forty days, then He ascended to heaven, in bodily form, whilst they looked on. The 'Son of Man' is now in heaven, representing all humanity, especially those who have believed in Him. He has entered the true temple of God, where He intercedes on our behalf before God. Although His glory is now restored, He retains His humanity, and is the ambassador of humankind in the heavenly realms for all time. He also serves as head of the entire body of believers who are living in the earthly realm. Stephen, who became the first Christian martyr, was full of the Holy Spirit when he gazed up at heaven and saw the glory of God with Jesus standing at His right hand. Stephen said, 'Behold, I see the heavens opened up and the Son of Man standing at the right hand of God' (see Acts 7:56).

There are many examples of God using the expression 'son of man' in a very general sense when He addressed His servants in the Old Testament. But in the book of Daniel the term is used very specifically to prophesy the return of Christ at the end of the age. Daniel wrote, 'In my visions at night I looked, and there was One like a Son of Man, coming with the clouds of heaven, and He came up to the Ancient of Days and was presented before Him. And to Him was given dominion, glory and a kingdom, that all the peoples, nations and men of every language might serve Him. His dominion is an everlasting dominion which will not pass away; And His kingdom is one which will not be destroyed' (see Daniel 7:13-14). Although Jesus referred to Himself using the term 'Son of Man' many times, the reference was ambiguous, because it was unclear whether He was claiming to be the 'Son of Man' Daniel spoke of, or simply a servant of God in the general sense. However, after He was arrested and the high priest asked Him whether He was the Messiah, He replied, 'I am. And you will see the Son of Man sitting at the right hand of power and coming with the clouds of heaven'. This was a very clear declaration that He is, indeed, the Son of Man of Daniel's visions, who is to return.

11 ¶ CHRIST REINTRODUCES US TO HIS FATHER

Jesus was very clear in explaining the loving nature of the Father, which includes calling Jesus' followers children of God. In the guidelines Jesus gave for prayer we see that the Father's concern for His children extends to every detail of our lives: 'When you pray, go into your inner room, close your door and pray to your Father who is in secret, and your Father who sees what is done in secret will reward you. And when you are praying, do not use meaningless repetition as the Gentiles do, for they suppose that they will be heard for their many words. So do not be like them; for your Father knows what you need before you ask Him. Pray, then, in this way: Our Father…' (Matthew 6:6-9 NASB). The word 'our' means that the heavenly Father we are praying to is Jesus' Father, and He is also the Father of all humanity. After Jesus had risen from the dead, He told Mary 'I am ascending to My Father and your Father, and My God and your God' (John 20:17). This shows Jesus raises His followers to His standing, as children of God, just as He humbles Himself to our level, as a servant of God: 'I am among you as one who serves' (Luke 22:27). And, through faith, this is what He has made us—precious children, with access to our heavenly Father whenever we desire to come to Him.

Christ has clearly stated how He has reconnected us with His Father: Jesus said, 'I am the way and the truth and the life. No one comes to the Father except through Me. If you know Me, you will know My Father also. From now on, you do know Him and have seen Him.' (John 14:6). He also promised, 'Whoever has My commandments and keeps them is the one who loves Me. And the ones who love Me will be loved by My Father, and I will love them and show Myself to them.' (John 14:21). Christ told His followers that our relationship with the Father would become closer as He returned to heaven: 'I am not saying that I will ask the

Father on your behalf, for the Father Himself loves you because you have loved Me and have believed that I came from God. I came from the Father and entered the world; now I am leaving the world and going back to the Father.' (John 16:26-28 NIV). Shortly before He died, Christ asked the Father to protect His disciples and all future believers: 'I have revealed You to the people whom You gave Me out of the world. They were Yours and You gave them to Me and they have obeyed Your word. Now they know that everything You have given Me is from You; for I gave them the words You gave Me and they accepted them. They knew with certainty that I came from You, and they believed that You sent Me. I pray for them. I am not praying for the world, but for those You have given Me, for they are Yours. All I have is Yours, and all You have is Mine. And glory has come to Me through them. I will remain in the world no longer, but they are still in the world, and I am coming to You. Holy Father, protect them by the power of Your name, the name You gave Me, so that they may be one as We are one' (John 17:6-11 NIV). Believers are reunited with Father God now, and for eternity.

***

12 ¶ CHRIST WILLINGLY GAVE HIS LIFE FOR US

It was with sober presence of mind that Christ gave His life for humanity: 'I lay down My life in order that I may take it back again. No one is taking it away from

Me but I lay it down of My own free will. I have the power to lay it down, and I have the power to take it up again' (John 10:17-18). Jesus could have saved Himself from being beaten and crucified at any moment throughout His sufferings: 'I could appeal to My Father, and at once He would put at My disposal more than twelve legions of angels. But then how would the Scriptures be fulfilled which say it must happen this way?' (Matthew 26: 53-54). But He chose, and kept on choosing, to submit to the ordeal. Every detail of His suffering was necessary for undoing the consequences of Adam's sin, and for establishing a way to reconnect humankind with the Father.

Even when He was hanging on the cross Jesus kept a clear head because He was determined to be led by the Holy Spirit to His last breath. Everything He said from the cross was for the sake of other people. He gave His mother and the disciple John to one another; He gave eternal life to a repentant criminal crucified next to Him; He quoted the first line of Psalm 22—which prophetically describes the details of the crucifixion—in order to trigger in the minds of the religious experts the entire psalm, which was being fulfilled before their very eyes: 'I am poured out like water, and all my bones are out of joint. My heart has turned to wax; it has melted within me. My mouth is dried up like a potsherd, and my tongue sticks to the roof of my mouth; you lay me in the dust of death. Dogs surround me, a pack of villains encircles me; they pierce my hands and my feet. All my bones are on display; people stare and gloat over me. They divide my clothes among them and cast lots for my garment' (Psalm 22:14-18 NIV).

Before the soldiers crucified Jesus they offered Him a drink of 'wine mixed with gall', but gall represents bitterness, and He refused to drink it (see Matthew 27:34). However, right at the end of His ordeal Jesus called for a drink: 'After this Jesus, knowing that all was now accomplished, so that the Scripture would be fulfilled, said, "I am thirsty." A jar full of sour wine was there, so they attached a sponge soaked in the sour wine to a stalk of hyssop and held it to His mouth. When He had taken the sour wine, Jesus said, "It is accomplished." And He bowed His head and handed over His spirit' (John 19:28-30 Mounce). This last act was also quite deliberate. Jesus died with His teeth set on edge by the sour wine, which fulfils the promise given in both Jeremiah 18 and Ezekiel 31. Both these prophets declared God's promise of a new covenant, in which the sins of the fathers would no longer be visited on the children, to the third and fourth generation (see Numbers 14:18): 'In those days they shall no longer say, "The fathers have eaten sour grapes, and the children's teeth are set on edge." But every one shall die for his own iniquity; every man who eats sour grapes, his own teeth shall be set on edge. "Behold, the days are coming, says the Lord, when I will make a new covenant..."' (Jeremiah 31:29-34). 'The Lord God says, "As surely as I live, you shall no longer use this proverb in Israel"'

(Ezekiel 18:3). 'The soul who sins shall die. The son shall not bear the guilt of the father, nor the father bear the guilt of the son' (Ezekiel 18:20 NKJV). Through His death on the cross Jesus not only established an antidote for the sins of those who put their trust in Him, but He also provides a means of liberation from the insidious effects of ancestral sins in believers' lives. Thus Christ has overthrown the devil's power to harm believers through this covert strategy.

Jesus understood precisely the degree to which He would suffer when He went to the cross. He had no trace of self-pity, He had unmatched courage and determination, and He completely and successfully finished the work He came to do.

---

13 ¶ CHRIST TOOK THE CONSEQUENCES OF OUR SIN

Sinful behaviours have harmful effects on ourselves and others. However, the work of Christ has established, once and for all, the capacity to reverse the destructive impact of sin. His work exposes the activities of Satan, who deals in death—in other words, when people are deceived by his suggestions, they later receive deadly consequences. However, Christ has provided the solution for all who want it: 'The Son of Man did not come to be served, but to serve, and to give His life as a ransom for many' (Mark 10:45). And Peter also explains, 'You know that you were ransomed from the futile ways inherited from your fathers, not with perishable things such as silver or gold, but with the precious blood of Christ, like that of a lamb without blemish or spot' (1 Peter 1:18-19 RSV).

God abhors the shedding of human blood, and has therefore never required a human sacrifice. As God explained, 'They have filled this place with the blood of the innocent, burning their sons in the fire as burnt offerings, something which I never commanded or spoke of, nor did it ever enter My mind' (see Jeremiah 19:4-5). However, as a result of the fall, Satan has sometimes managed to convince humanity that human sacrifice was the right way to appease 'the gods'. Yet it is Satan who has the bloodlust, because he sees human beings as potential friends of God, and thus his own enemies. Since Satan sets the rules of this fallen world system (see John 12:31), and deceives humanity into engaging with it, it is his rules that require human blood as a trading medium. Christ had to be incarnated as a human being, in the midst of this world system, to deposit His own innocent blood as an antidote to the control of Satan. This antidote is available for all who trust in Him. By doing this, He has 'overcome the world' (see John 16:33).

The first Adam was deceived by the serpent (Satan) into eating the fruit of the tree of the knowledge of good-and-evil. By submitting to Satan's suggestion, Adam relinquished the authority God gave him to rule over the earth, and Satan took up this authority. Thus,

Satan adjudicates with his own version of good and bad. He induces people to sin, and then accuses them, according to his twisted law. The tree of the knowledge of good-and-evil is thus Satan's domain, yet the tree of life continues to be God's domain. After the fall, God prevented Adam and Eve from eating of the tree of life, stationing the cherubim and the flaming sword to block their entrance to the Garden of Eden (see Genesis 3:24).

In due time, Christ was incarnated as the last Adam, and as such it was necessary for Him to enter into the world system itself, and to come under its rules, in order to release its captives, from the inside. Christ's death and resurrection enables human beings to switch systems, and ultimately to access the tree of life. In fact, one of the earliest and most straightforward explanations of the atonement, widely accepted for the first thousand years of Christianity, is the 'ransom theory'. This theory reasons that Jesus, being Himself God, did not pay a ransom to Himself. Hence, it is argued, Jesus gave His own blood as the 'ransom money' to pay into Satan's system for the release of human beings from his bondage. The early Christians understood that the primary purpose of the cross was to defeat Satan's schemes. This accords with Jesus' declared mandate: 'The Spirit of the Lord is upon Me, because He has anointed Me to proclaim good news to the poor. He has sent Me to proclaim freedom to the captives and recovery of sight to the blind, to set the oppressed free, to proclaim the year of the Lord's favour' (Luke 4:18-19). Thus Jesus has made provision for the enslaving consequences of human sin.

---

14 ¶ CHRIST REMOVES OUR SENSE OF CONDEMNATION

If we focus on religious law in our mind we become conscious of our failings, and we feel shame. The law does not have the power to help us change our behaviour, only to make us feel bad about our behaviour. Sometimes the law can even awaken our propensities, as Paul experienced: 'I would not have come to know sin except through the Law; for I would not have known about coveting if the Law had not said, "You shall not covet." But sin, taking opportunity through the commandment, produced in me coveting of every kind; for apart from the Law sin is dead' (Romans 7:7-8 NASB). The problem Paul identifies here is that he started to try not to covet, and failed miserably. In order to conform to the law a person has to focus on himself, and what he needs to do, but Jesus' work on the cross has provided us with an alternative to religious law—focusing on Christ, who has already done everything necessary to fulfil the requirements of the law. For the believer, the feeling of condemnation thus acts as a 'thermometer' showing us we have shifted our focus back onto law. But this also acts in our favour because it reminds us to focus on Christ again. As Paul explains, he fully agrees with God's laws in his mind, but his body resonates with a different law which conflicts with the Law of God, taking him captive to the law of sin: 'How wretched I am! How can I get free from this body of death? Thank God—through Jesus Christ our Lord! So, now there is no condemnation for those in Christ Jesus, because the law of the Spirit of life in Christ Jesus has set us free from the law of sin and of death. The Law required human effort to fulfil it, but was never able to rescue us from our sinful nature, because it merely regulates outward behaviour, and has no bearing on our inner attitudes of heart. Therefore God sent His own Son in the likeness of sinful flesh and as an offering for sin, condemning sin in the flesh, so that the justification of the Law is complete in us, as we walk according to the Spirit' (see Romans 7:22-8:4). The tussle which Paul is describing here demonstrates the inner conflict that arises from human nature that is under the influence of the tree of the knowledge of good and evil. However, Christ has given believers an alternative way to live, which emanates from the Spirit of life, and thereby He removes our sense of condemnation.

15 ¶ CHRIST HAS BEEN GIVEN THE AUTHORITY TO JUDGE

It is not the Father who judges, but Christ. Jesus says: 'Just as the Father raises the dead and gives them life, likewise the Son also gives life to those He chooses. The Father judges no one but has given all judgment to the

Son, so that all will honour the Son, as they honour the Father. The one who hears My word and believes Him who sent Me has eternal life and will not come into judgment, but has passed from death to life' (see John 5:21-24). Passing from death to life means that believers' transgressions, and their consequences, have been removed from the records.

However, the bible is clear that there will be a final judgment by Christ, who has earned the right to conduct this process through living a human life: 'Nothing in creation is hidden from God's sight. Everything is uncovered and exposed before the eyes of Him to whom we must give account. Now, we have a great high priest who has ascended into heaven, Jesus the Son of God, and we hold on to our profession of faith. For our high priest is able to empathise with our weaknesses, because He has been tempted in every way, just as we are, yet He did not sin' (Hebrews 4:12-15). 'Everyone must appear before the judgment seat of Christ so that each one may be repayed for his deeds in the body, whether good or bad' (2 Corinthians 5:10). Believers will be rewarded by Christ for deeds carried out that conform to His will. On the other hand, people who have ultimately chosen to reject the offer of forgiveness, and who want God to leave them alone, will be eternally separated from God.

Some are troubled by the thought that if a person is born into a culture where the Christian gospel is never heard, or is forbidden, what then will be the eternal destiny of that person? If salvation is by grace alone, and thus not from human effort, on what grounds could those people be excluded? We find some resolution to this uncomfortable question in the little known statement written by the apostle Peter: 'For Christ also died for sins once for all, the just for the unjust, so that He might bring us to God, having been put to death in the flesh, but made alive in the spirit; in which also He went and made proclamation to the spirits now in prison, who once were disobedient, when the patience of God kept waiting in the days of Noah, during the construction of the ark, in which a few, that is, eight persons, were brought safely through the water' (1 Peter 3:18-20 NASB). From this statement we are led to understand that after His resurrection, Christ went to the people who had died in the flood which destroyed the world, and proclaimed the gospel to them. This does not refer to Noah and his family, but rather was for the sake of the people who were disobedient, whose spirits were held captive up to that point. This gives an indication of the fairness of God, and is supported by the fact that He does not want any to perish. His ways are mysterious, but He is kind and loving to all, and He takes into consideration all the circumstances, experiences and deceptions which people have been subjected to. Therefore we can be confident that His judgments are merciful, since mercy triumphs over judgment (see James 2:13).

However, although God is merciful, people who are

still under the deception of Satan at the time of Christ's return will be terrified by the prospect: 'The kings of the earth and the great men and the commanders and the rich and the strong and every slave and free man hid themselves in the caves and among the rocks of the mountains; and they said to the mountains and to the rocks, "Fall on us and hide us from the presence of Him who sits on the throne, and from the wrath of the Lamb; for the great day of their wrath has come, and who is able to stand?"' (Revelation 6:15-17 NASB). Jesus explained that 'the Son of Man' will come in His glory and will judge every person, from all the nations, based on their response to others who were in need, as if the needy one had been Jesus Himself. If a person's response was compassionate, they will be rewarded. But if their response was to harden their heart and ignore other's needs, they will suffer loss (see Matthew 25:31-46).

16 ¶ CHRIST GIVES US ETERNAL LIFE

As a result of Christ dying on the cross and His resurrection, believers gain an eternal destiny that will be far better than any passing pleasure of this world: 'No eye has seen, nor ear has heard, nor has the human mind imagined the things that God has prepared for those who love Him' (1 Corinthians 2:9 Mounce). Often people cannot conceive of life which continues forever, and imagine it would be tedious. But the scripture promises something entirely different from our lives in this world.

The experience of eternal life begins when the believer first encounters Christ, as Jesus told the woman at the well: 'Everyone who drinks this water will thirst again, but whoever drinks the water I give him shall never thirst; because the water I give will become a spring of water flowing out to eternal life within him' (John 4:13-14). Christ teaches that the gift of eternal life is irrevocable: 'My sheep hear My voice, and I know them, and they follow Me; and I give eternal life to them, and they will never perish; and no one will snatch them out of My hand. My Father, who has given them to Me, is greater than all; and no one is able to snatch them out of the Father's hand' (John 10:27-29 NASB).

And in the age to come, believers will have access to the tree of life. In his visions on the island of Patmos, John was given a glimpse of the city in heaven: An angel showed him a river of the water of life, clear as crystal, flowing from the throne of God and of the Lamb, along the middle of the city's street. On both sides of the river was the tree of life, bearing twelve kinds of fruit, bearing fruit every month; and its leaves were for the healing of the nations. There is no curse and the throne of God and of the Lamb is in the city, and His servants will serve Him; they will see His face, and His name will be on their foreheads (Revelation 22:1-4).

3

OUR RELATIONSHIP WITH CHRIST

17. He has awakened us to our spiritual identity
18. He has given us the mind of Christ
19. He shall have us with Him forever
20. He has given us peace with Him
21. He is in us and we are in Him
22. He lives in us and we live in Him
23. He is our brother and friend
24. He continuously works on our behalf

17 ¶ HE HAS AWAKENED US TO OUR SPIRITUAL IDENTITY

Believers, by nature, are spiritually awakened. An important consequence of our faith in Christ is that we are now reconnected with God in a new form of relationship that enables us to discern the difference between our soul and spirit. The difference between the soul and spirit is often a source of confusion amongst believers, yet the distinction is clearly made in the scriptures (see 1 Thessalonians 5:23 and Hebrews 4:12). It is our conviction that the soul is associated with our human mind, which is where our reasoning, intuition, imagination, instincts, will and emotions are processed. The human spirit, on the other hand, is associated with the mystical or unseen dimension, and in particular, God who is Spirit. In this conception, our spiritual experiences are not only internal, because they are received in our awakened human spirit and thereafter perceived in our soul, but they are also external since they derive from the unseen heavenly realm—the throne of God. Thus when Simon Peter was asked who he thought Jesus was, he responded by saying: 'You are the Christ the Son of the living God' (Matthew 16:16 NIV) and Jesus commended him, stating, 'blessed are you Simon son of Jonah, for this was not revealed to you by man, but by My Father in heaven' (Matthew 16:17 NIV), thus showing that Peter was awakened to God.

The fact that we now have faith is evidence that we have 'heard' from God, and since God is spirit this suggests that whatever we hear from God is spiritually discerned, that is, received in our human spirit rather than conceived in our mind. Thereafter, the things God reveals to our spirit are perceived and processed through the filter of the conscious and subliminal mind.

At first, the spiritual is in contradiction to our soul, since the soul thinks differently from the mind of God. But with divine revelation, through grace, the soul is itself transformed by the act of processing the spiritual activity—which results in the renewing of the mind. The important point is that the spirit instigates, and the soul responds. The Virgin Mary, for example, said: 'My soul magnifies the Lord, and my spirit has rejoiced in God my Saviour' (Luke 1:46-47 NKJV). In this instance, the magnifying of the Lord by Mary's soul is only possible due to the revelation already received in her spirit, by grace. In a similar way, Christ has awakened believers to their spiritual identity.

18 ¶ He has given us the mind of Christ

As believers, we have been given the mind of Christ, although it is progressively disclosed to us by the reordering of our mind. We are encouraged to cooperate with this process, by offering up to God our opinions, perspectives and positions, including our theology: 'Do not be conformed to this world, but be transformed by the renewing of your mind, so that you may discern the will of God, which is good and acceptable and perfect' (Romans 12:2). As in Jesus' incarnation, His mind was constantly in tune with the Father, the Holy Spirit helps believers to fix our attention on His priorities, and not have our thoughts hijacked by fruitless distractions: 'Now we have received, not the spirit of the world, but the Spirit who is from God, so that we may know the things freely given to us by God, which things we also speak, not in words taught by human wisdom, but in those taught by the Spirit, combining spiritual thoughts with spiritual words. But a soulish person does not accept the things of the Spirit of God, for they are foolishness to him; and he cannot understand them, because they are spiritually appraised. But he who is spiritual appraises all things, yet he himself is appraised by no one. For who has known the mind of the Lord, that he will instruct Him? But we have the mind of Christ' (1 Corinthians 2:12-16 NASB). In addition, as our minds are renewed, fear loses its hold over us: 'God has not given us a spirit of fear, but of power and of love and of a sound mind' (2 Timothy 1:7). It is sometimes said that believers can be 'too heavenly minded to be any earthly good', but this is a misconception. The problem is that we are usually not heavenly minded enough, because in fact the mind of Christ is continuously earth focussed, as we see in the way Jesus taught His disciples to pray: 'Your Kingdom come, Your will be done on earth, as it is in heaven' (Matthew 6:10).

While He was on earth, Christ fully embraced His human vulnerability, understanding that, of Himself, He could do nothing. He lived a life of surrender to the will of the Father, by the Spirit of God: 'Not by might, nor by power, but by My Spirit' (Zechariah 4:6). Although He existed in the form of God, He did not consider equality with God something to be held on to, emptying Himself in order to become the Son of Man, and He continuously relinquished His human strength and sufficiency in order to rely entirely on the Spirit. God also taught Paul this principle when Paul prayed for relief from his torment, telling him, 'My grace is sufficient for you, for power is perfected in weakness.' Paul understood that his torment had the specific purpose of stopping him from becoming conceited. He therefore embraced his own vulnerability so that he could freely draw upon the grace of God: 'I am happy to boast about my weaknesses so that the power of Christ may dwell in me. I am content with weaknesses, with insults, with hardship, with persecutions, with difficulties, for the sake of Christ, for when I am weak, then I am strong' (see 2 Corinthians 12:9-10). Because believers have the mind of Christ they are able to embrace their vulnerability, to defer to the Spirit of God and to understand the situations they are facing from God's perspective.

19 ¶ He shall have us with Him forever

Christ desires the presence of His followers with Him in paradise, so that they will also experience the wonders He enjoys.

There is much confusion in people's thinking regarding heaven. In western cultures we are taught the myth of Santa Claus, almost from our birth. On the surface this seems like a harmless white lie which stimulates children's imagination and wonder. But there is a message attached to the myth that affects people's perception of heaven: Children are taught that if they have been good, Santa Claus will reward them with a Christmas present, but if they have been naughty they will receive nothing. This establishes a pattern of thinking that good behaviour will be rewarded. So later in life, many people believe they will 'go to heaven' when they die because they have been good, without any reference to a relationship with God. And yet Jesus gives a different message. For example, the thief who was dying on the cross next to Him had been a bad person all his life. He had no opportunity to go and make amends, or start living a reformed life. And yet, when he asked Jesus to 'remember me when you come into your kingdom', indicating that this criminal believed who Jesus was, and put his trust in Him, Jesus declared that 'today you will be with Me in paradise'. From the gospels it is clear that paradise itself means dwelling in the presence of Jesus, and this prospect is the believer's joy.

Jesus told Pontius Pilate: 'My kingdom is not of this world'. Christ was not incarnated in order to take over the rulership of the earth, but rather He chose to pay the highest price so that He would get the best possible outcome—for us and for Himself. He was willing to be put to death by crucifixion, despite its agony and shame, so that He could have us with Him in paradise forever. In fact Jesus had great joy in anticipation of returning to His Father: 'If you loved Me you would be glad I am going to the Father' (John 14:28). He wants us with Him in the realm of eternity, where Father God dwells. Therefore, before the crucifixion, Christ interceded in prayer on our behalf: 'Father, I desire that they also, whom You have given Me, be with Me where I am, so that they may see My glory which You have given Me, for You loved Me before the foundation of the world' (John 17:24 NASB). Through the Spirit of God we are able to commune with Christ before we physically die. Then, when we die, and in the age to come, we shall enjoy unbroken fellowship with Him.

***

20 ¶ He has given us peace with Him

Christ gives believers peace. When Jesus announced that He would shortly die, the disciples were upset and bewildered, but Jesus promised them, 'Peace I leave with you; My peace I give to you; I am not giving to you as the world gives. Do not let your heart be troubled, nor let it be fearful' (John 14:27). This peace is not simply a sensory experience, but it is a supernatural resource that is given by Christ to those who have faith: 'Now that we are justified by faith we have peace with God through our Lord Jesus Christ' (Romans 5:1). For instance, in times of distress or suffering we can experience His spiritual peace, which calms our heart and mind despite our circumstances: 'And the peace of God, which transcends all understanding, will guard your hearts and your minds in Christ Jesus' (Philippians 4:7 NIV).

However, it is not the intention of God to enable people to find real peace apart from Him. The existence of discomfort is not cruelty by the Creator—rather, it encourages non-believers to seek alleviation from their distress, and as they do so, to find the Prince of Peace, Christ Himself. But Christ did not come to bring peace to the world system, which remains subjected to the deceptions of the fall. Instead He rescues people from that system. Jesus said: 'Do not suppose that I have come to bring peace to the earth. I did not come to bring peace, but a sword' (Matthew 10:34 NIV). The sword Jesus speaks of is not a call to arms, as the crusaders misinterpreted it, but refers to the enmity between the Kingdom of God and Satan's realm. It is having the Kingdom of God within us that gives us peace.

---

21 ¶ HE IS IN US AND WE ARE IN HIM

Christ is in believers. Just before He was crucified, Jesus petitioned His Father on behalf of His followers, 'My prayer is not for them alone. I pray also for those who will believe in Me through their message, that all of them may be one, Father, just as You are in Me and I am in You. May they also be in Us so that the world may believe that You have sent Me. I have given them the glory that You gave Me, that they may be one as We are one—I in them and You in Me—so that they may be brought to complete unity' (John 17:20-23 NIV). This common unity that Christ refers to here is a spiritual unity, not one based on compatibility of personality or culture. We can safely assume that God the Father has answered Jesus' request, and therefore believers' unity is not only a possibility, but a spiritual reality.

God commissioned Paul to explain to new believers the extraordinary phenomenon of Christ's presence within them as a reality, and the living hope of being with Him forever. He understood his ministry as a stewardship given to him by God to explain the mystery, that was hidden for ages and generations, but has been revealed to His saints. 'God has chosen to reveal to believers what are the riches of the glory of this mystery among the nations: which is Christ in you, the hope of glory' (Colossians 1:27). Thus, being in Christ and having Christ in us, relates to the believers' identity, and their unity.

22 ¶ HE LIVES IN US AND WE LIVE IN HIM

Christ said to the disciples: 'I am the vine; you are the branches. The one who abides in me and I in him bears much fruit, for apart from me you can do nothing. If anyone does not abide in me, he is like a branch that is thrown away and withers; men gather them and throw them into the fire, and they are burned. If you abide in me and my words abide in you, ask whatever you wish and it will be done for you. My Father is glorified in this, that you bear much fruit and become my disciples' (John 15:5-8 Mounce). In the original context Jesus is pointing out that the branches attached to a vine will bear grapes, but the branches that have been cut off cannot bear any grapes because they are disconnected from their source of life. In a similar way, disciples will bear fruit for God's glory if they stay connected to their source of life—and this is precisely what God desires. This scripture alludes to disciples living their lives led by the Holy Spirit, as Jesus Himself did. As His followers do this, as well as becoming Christlike, they bring the presence of God wherever they are sent, they love one another, and they experience joy and the Father's love, as Jesus also did. Thus, living in Christ and having Christ live in us, relates to the believers' conduct, and their destiny.

23 ¶ HE IS OUR BROTHER AND FRIEND

Christ is glad to welcome believers into His family. Whilst Jesus was speaking to a group of people someone came and told Him that His mother and brothers were standing outside waiting to speak to Him. But Jesus' response was, 'Who is My mother and who are My brothers?'. Then, pointing over at His disciples, He said, 'Look, these are My mother and My brothers, because whoever does the will of My Father who is in heaven is My brother and sister and mother' (Matthew 12:47-50). Christ considers us all to be His family because we have acted in faith by believing in Him, which is Father God's desire: On one occasion some people asked Jesus, 'What are the things that God wants us to do?' Jesus explained, 'This is what God requires, that you believe in Him whom He has sent' (see John 6:28-29).

Christ also calls us His friends when we respond to His will, and He shares the mysteries of heaven with us in order that we can engage with His purpose: 'Greater love has no one than this, that one lay down his life for his friends. You are My friends if you do what I command you. No longer do I call you slaves, for the slave does not know what his master is doing; but I have called you friends, for all things that I have heard from My Father I have made known to you' (John 15:13-15 NASB). Naturally when we choose friends, we look for people we prefer, or who are like us, or through whom we gain some prestige by association. When we are let down by friends we quickly ditch them. Jesus, however, does not offer His friendship for what He can get out of the relationship, as we do, but for what He can give. Christ takes the initiative to be a friend to people and makes Himself vulnerable and transparent to them, even to Judas Iscariot whom Jesus greeted as a friend as He was being betrayed.

---

24 ¶ He continuously works on our behalf

Although Christ has completed His work on the earth, He continues to work on behalf of believers. We are considered as perfect because we have believed in Christ, and our act of believing is counted as righteousness: God spoke to Abraham and promised him something way beyond the realms of possibility. Yet Abraham was absolutely convinced that God was able to fulfil what He had promised. God equated Abraham's faith as righteousness. This incident set a spiritual precedent whereby all those who hear God and believe what He says will be reckoned as righteous. This applies to all who believe in Him who raised Jesus our Lord from the dead (see Romans 4:21-24). But despite the fact that we are considered righteous, Christ is still working for us because we continue to make mistakes, and our thinking needs correcting. This is the provision of the new covenant, which is contrasted with the old: 'When Jesus, our High Priest, had offered one sacrifice for sins for all time, He sat down at the right hand of God, and since that time He waits for His enemies to be made His footstool. By one sacrifice He has made perfect forever those who are being made holy' (Hebrews 10:11-14). Jesus has sat down at the right hand of the Father; this expression indicates completion of the work of redemption. However, now in heaven as our great High Priest, Jesus continues to speak on our behalf in the courts of heaven, and to request the spiritual resources for us, who are still living in this world, with all its pitfalls and trials. 'For Christ did not enter a sanctuary made with human hands that was only a copy of the true one; He entered heaven itself, now to appear for us in God's presence' (Hebrews 9:24 NIV). Jesus has not only dealt with our past sins through His death and resurrection, but He has also made provision for the sins we might commit as believers: 'My dear children, I write this to you so that you will not sin. But if anybody does sin, we have an advocate with the Father—Jesus Christ, the Righteous One. He is the atoning sacrifice for our sins, and not only for ours but also for the sins of the whole world' (1 John 2:1-2 NIV).

The book of Hebrews gives an excellent explanation of how Jesus completed the requirements of the old covenant, and instigated the new priesthood of which we are all part, with Jesus as our great High Priest: 'It is clear that our Lord is descended from Judah, and nobody from that tribe serves in the Levitical priesthood. If however another priest arises according to the likeness of Melchizedek, His priestly status does not originate from His tribe, but on the basis of having an indestructible life. For in Psalm 110 David writes that the Lord has vowed to Jesus: "You are a priest for all time, according to the order of Melchizedek." Because

Jesus lives forever He has a permanent priesthood. Therefore, He is able to save completely those who come to God through Him, because He always lives to intercede for them (see Hebrews 7:14-25). Christ has already invested so much in believers, and He is completely committed to seeing them 'finish the race', therefore He continues to work on their behalf.

4

OUR IDENTITY IN CHRIST

25. We receive revelation that we are children of God
26. We were born for a purpose on earth
27. We have become a new creation
28. We are a people of faith
29. We have had our sins rendered irrelevant
30. We have rest from religious obligation
31. We carry the fragrance of Christ
32. We can partake of His nature

25 ¶ WE RECEIVE REVELATION THAT WE ARE CHILDREN OF GOD

Believers in Christ receive a new identity, by revelation: 'See what great love the Father has lavished on us, that we should be called children of God! And that is what we are! The reason the world does not know us is that it did not know Him. Dear friends, now we are children of God, and what we will be has not yet been made known. But we know that when Christ appears, we shall be like Him, for we shall see Him as he is' (1 John 3:1-2 NIV). Because we are God's children we are aware that we are being lovingly parented, and we are encouraged to respond accordingly: 'Do all things without grumbling or disputing; so that you will prove yourselves to be blameless and innocent, children of God above reproach in the midst of a crooked and perverse generation, among whom you appear as lights in the world' (Philippians 2:14-15 NASB).

God uses all our circumstances, enjoyable or unpleasant, to make us fit for the destiny He has prepared for us. Even in the busyness of every day life the Holy Spirit makes us aware of our identity as God's children, and helps us keep our focus on eternity: 'The Spirit Himself testifies with our spirit that we are God's children. Now if we are children, then we are heirs— heirs of God and co-heirs with Christ, if indeed we share in His sufferings in order that we may also share in His glory' (Romans 8:16-17 NASB).

26 ¶ WE WERE BORN FOR A PURPOSE ON EARTH

Since human beings have a spirit which belongs to God in the first place, and which goes back to Him when we die, what is the point of our life on earth? Why do we have to go through all the suffering and temptation associated with life in this corrupted world? We believe there is purpose in our own 'incarnation'. We are not referring here to destiny, as in each person having tasks to fulfil on earth which may be either quenched, distorted, perverted or achieved, depending on a person's environment, connectedness with God, or their decisions.

With the notion of 'purpose', we refer to the nature of our creature-hood, that is to say, we are created as vulnerable, fallible, and mortal. Every person will die; anyone could be a victim of tragedy; anyone could be a perpetrator of evil. The one thing human beings control is their own choices, even though these may be very limited. But the human spirit, which comes from God, also longs for God, so there is hope for every person.

When people are misled by Satan they can imagine themselves to be powerful, infallible, and immortal—which is deception. We know God does not want anyone to perish, but many people put their trust in themselves and believe they do not need God. However, human weakness and powerlessness are often the cause of people crying out to God—who will respond by making Himself a reality to such people. Thus, the very weakness built in to the human race can drive people to question the nature of this world and the meaning of life. Through this way of humility many have found access to the treasure of heaven, which is God Himself.

The purpose of our incarnation is to discover God—despite the fact that we have not been in His presence as the angels have, and we have not seen His glory: 'Though you have not seen Him, you love Him; and even though you do not see Him now, you believe in Him and are filled with an inexpressible and glorious joy, for you are receiving the end result of your faith, the salvation of your souls' (1 Peter 1:8-9 NIV). God is pleased when people find Him, through Jesus, and He will reward them when their life ends: 'Through His great mercy God has given us new birth into a living hope through the resurrection of Jesus Christ from the dead. We have an inheritance which is reserved in heaven for us, pure and undefiled, beyond the reach of change and decay. And through faith you are protected by the power of God for salvation, which is ready to be revealed in the last time.' (1 Peter 1:3-5). The reason human beings have been created is so they can discover, know and learn to trust God, who loves them. Christ has enabled us to find the ultimate purpose for which we are born.

---

27 ¶ WE HAVE BECOME A NEW CREATION

When believers first encounter Christ and are then awakened to their new spiritual being, they discover that there is power available to live differently: 'Therefore if anyone is in Christ, there is a new creation;

what is old has passed away; behold, what is new has come!' (2 Corinthians 5:17 Mounce). Our spiritual destiny is new to us, but was in the mind of God before He created the earth: 'The God and Father of our Lord Jesus Christ has blessed us with every spiritual blessing in the heavenly places in Christ, just as He chose us in Him before the foundation of the world, that we would be holy and blameless before Him' (Ephesians 1:3-4).

Paul teaches believers how the work of Christ has impacted him, and how God has removed all worldly divisions in His new creation: 'Through the cross of our Lord Jesus Christ the world has been crucified to me, and I to the world. Neither circumcision nor uncircumcision means anything; all that counts is the new creation' (Galatians 6:14-15).

Paul further encourages believers to live their lives from this newly created self: 'With regard to your former way of life, put off your old self, which is corrupted by its deceitful desires, and be renewed in the spirit of your minds; and put on the new self, created in God's likeness in true righteousness and holiness' (Ephesians 4:22-24). It is interesting that in this scripture the desires of our 'old self' are called deceitful, because this suggests that as we become aware of the truth of our new creation identity, our desires will progressively be transformed.

28 ¶ WE ARE A PEOPLE OF FAITH

Believers, by definition, are a people of faith. Indeed, it was faith that secured their entry into the Kingdom of God. In our modern context the word 'faith' is generally used to mean three things: trust in someone's good character, adherence to a religious grouping, or strong belief in religious doctrine. In the context of the New Testament, however, the word 'faith' (Greek: pistis) is very specific: 'Faith is the assurance of things hoped for, the conviction of things not seen' (Hebrews 11:1). People do not gain faith by determination, or by repeatedly speaking out a promise from the bible, like a mantra. The bible is very clear that faith comes through hearing God speak to you personally: 'Faith comes from hearing, and hearing through the word of Christ' (Romans 10:17). In this passage the Greek 'rhema', translated as 'word', is a personally revealed word. As soon as a believer has truly heard God say something, they can never thereafter doubt or disbelieve what they have heard. Faith is not learnt from human beings, but is the result of revelation. A person may hear a biblical truth taught in church for years, and give mental assent to it. But if one day that person receives revelation from God about this same truth, there is an internalised consciousness of its reality. As faith is a gift from God, emanating from revelation, having too little faith is not a problem because we can seek God for more revelation in any situation.

In the book of Acts we read how a Pharisee named

Saul had the conviction that he was serving God by persecuting Christians. Then God gave him revelation whilst on his way to Damascus, and in that moment he was transformed; he knew he was wrong, he knew the true nature of God, and he knew his destiny was to make Christ known (see Acts 26:9-18). Not only the case of this pharisee, Saul, but also church history shows us the difference between doctrine and revelation: doctrine is something a person agrees with in the mind, and maybe they are willing even to kill to defend it; revelation is something that has entered a person's spirit, and maybe they are willing even to die to defend it. When God gives us revelation, it shows us something we did not previously know, or corrects something we were wrong about. Therefore we are in no position to criticise anyone who has not received that revelation. Thus, revelation should make believers humble rather than proud, and our response could well be 'What else can you show me, Father? What else am I wrong about?'. Therefore, humility and hunger to know more of God's ways go hand in hand.

---

29 ¶ WE HAVE HAD OUR SINS RENDERED IRRELEVANT

Christ has cast our sin to the other side of the universe: 'As far as the east is from the west, so far has He removed our transgressions from us' (Psalm 103:12). Sin is the expression—in word, deed, or thought—of the human soul that is independent of God. As Paul writes: 'whatever is not from faith is sin' (Romans 14:23). This statement seems alarming until you fit it together with the bible's definition of faith. Faith comes through hearing, and this hearing through the 'rhema' (revealed to the individual) word of God, which is then acted upon. During His incarnation Christ was continuously guided by listening to His Father, as He explained: 'The Son can do nothing on His own, but only what He sees the Father doing' (John 5:19) and 'I have not spoken on my own initiative, but the Father, who sent me, has Himself commanded me what to say and what to speak' (John 12:49).

The New Testament word translated as 'sin' is the Greek 'hamartia', derived from an archer firing an arrow which misses the target. This illustrates what happens when believers act independently of God. Since it is 'those who are led by the Spirit of God who are the sons of God' (Romans 8:14) it follows that sons of God do not act independently of God. Thus when we are not acting in faith we are living in accord with the deception of the fall. After the flood, God commissioned Noah and his descendants to 'be fruitful and multiply, and fill the earth' (Genesis 9:1). However, people jointly decided to build a city for themselves with a tower whose top would reach up to heaven, and to make a name for themselves. They defied God's wishes for humanity, because they did not want to be scattered across the face of the earth' (Genesis 11:4). The people decided to act independently of God and put their own desires and ideas above His. Therefore God confused their one common language, giving them many different languages which forced them to separate from one another and to populate different regions of the world. The primary issue for God, in its simplest form, was that they were acting independently of Him, not giving Him any consideration whatsoever. God has always desired that humankind would take account of Him: 'Trust in the Lord with all your heart and do not lean on your own understanding. In all your ways acknowledge Him, and He will make your paths straight. Do not be wise in your own eyes; Fear the Lord and turn away from evil' (Proverbs 3:5-7). The church, which was birthed at the coming of the Holy Spirit on the day of Pentecost, was meant to live every day guided by the Holy Spirit. Whilst the 'accuser of the brethren' reminds people of what they have done wrong, even though they may have repented, the Holy Spirit convicts us at those times when we do act independently of God, but without accusation. He does this because He can see we are 'missing the target', or sinning, and He is pleased to set us straight again.

---

30 ¶ WE HAVE REST FROM RELIGIOUS OBLIGATION

When we believe, the Holy Spirit gives us access to the benefits gained by the finished work of Christ on the cross, and therefore we can rest from our own religious self-effort: 'The promise of entering His rest still stands, therefore let us be careful that none of us is found to have fallen short of it' (Hebrews 4:1). In other words, believers are warned not to slip back into self-effort to obtain righteousness, or God's favour: 'Those who still try to be justified by the law have been alienated from Christ; they have fallen away from grace' (Galatians 5:4). Jesus invited His followers to come to Him to obtain this rest: 'Come to Me, all who are weary and heavy-laden, and I will give you rest. Take My yoke upon you and learn from Me, for I am gentle and humble in heart, and you will find rest for your souls. For My yoke is easy and My burden is light' (Matthew 11:28-30 NASB). The expression, 'take on a yoke' referred to discipleship in the Jewish context, and signifies learning to become like one's Rabbi, in thought and deed. Today the Holy Spirit extends this invitation to all believers.

When people are unsure of God's goodness, kindness and love they might perform good deeds or participate in religious rituals to gain an imagined right to God's favour. Religious activities may soothe the inner longing of the human soul, but the relief is transient, and does not change us. These human efforts are driven by the internalised 'knowledge of good and evil' which operates through a sliding scale of behaviour from good to bad, making us feel proud if we have done the right thing, or shame if we have done wrong. This swing between hubris and self-loathing, each getting the upper hand in turn depending on our performance, is a form of slavery. This is transcended by the knowledge and the experience that God is good, that He loves us dearly, and He has our best interests at heart.

Jesus illustrates the difference between human thinking that emanates from the 'tree of the knowledge of good and evil' and thinking that is congruent with the 'tree of life', in His parable of the prodigal son (see Luke 15:11-31). The two sons in the story both represent behaviours driven by the tree of the knowledge of good and evil: the 'good' son who has slaved for his father in order to gain a reward, and the 'bad' son who has disrespected his father and believes he has lost all reward. We see that both are disconnected from the father, because they have completely wrong ideas about what he is like. This loss of trust in the Father is exactly what Adam and Eve experienced after they had eaten from the wrong tree. However, the father in Jesus' story exemplifies the true situation, as discerned by those who are sustained by the tree of life.

Like Father God, this father's love is unshakable and his motives are kind: he stares at the horizon day after day, longing to see his lost son returning home to him. He generously shares all he has with the son who stays home: 'you are always with me and everything I have is yours'. We can enter God's rest when we have revelation that Christ has done everything necessary for our eternal reconnection to God, and therefore we no longer have to perform, in any shape or form, to appease Father God, or to gain His approval.

---

31 ¶ WE CARRY THE FRAGRANCE OF CHRIST

Wherever believers go, they carry the spiritual fragrance of Christ, whether they are aware of it or not. A fragrance cannot be rationalised, that is to say, there is no logical argument for or against Chanel No. 5— people either like it or dislike it: 'Thanks be to God, who is always leading us in triumph in Christ, and through us is making known the fragrance of the knowledge of Him in every place. For we are an aroma of Christ to God among those who are being saved. Among those who are perishing we are a deadly fume that kills, but to the former we are a life-giving fragrance that brings life. And who is adequate for a ministry like this?' (2 Corinthians 2:14-16 Mounce). Regardless whether believers speak about their faith, some people will want to be in their company, whilst others will find believers odious for no particular reason.

The gospels record that on more than one occasion women poured perfume over Jesus' feet, and on His head. Each gospel account reveals an aspect of the fragrance of Christ: 'Mary took a pound of costly perfume made of pure nard, anointed Jesus' feet and wiped them with her hair. The house was filled with the fragrance of the perfume. But Judas Iscariot, one of His disciples (the one who was about to betray Him), said "Why was this perfume not sold for three hundred denarii and the money given to the poor." (He said this not because he cared about the poor, but because he was a thief; he kept the common purse and used to steal what was put into it). Jesus said, "Leave her alone. She bought it so that she might keep it for the day of my burial'" (John 12: 3-7 NRSV). In this gospel account, the act of pouring perfume on Jesus' feet was offensive to Judas, whose heart was set against Him. Thus, for Judas the fragrance was as the 'deadly fume that kills' because he was unwilling to respond to the life-changing grace Christ offered, which posed a threat to the deceptions he was clinging on to.

In Luke's gospel, the woman pours out the perfume because she knows her many sins are forgiven, and therefore she feels love for Him. This happened at a Pharisee's house where He was invited to dinner. In his heart this Pharisee criticised Jesus for allowing a sinful woman to make this gesture, so Jesus told him a parable to help him understand. He said, 'You did not anoint My head with oil, but she anointed My feet with perfume. Therefore I tell you, her many sins have been forgiven, as her great love has shown; but he who has been forgiven little, loves little' (Luke 7:46-47). In a different account in Mark's gospel, Jesus says that what the woman did will be included in the gospel, in memory of her: 'She has done what she could; she has anointed My body beforehand for the burial. Truly I say to you, wherever the gospel is preached in the whole world, what this woman has done will also be spoken of in memory of her' (Mark 14:8-9 NASB). In the above scripture the woman was willing to be misunderstood and criticised for demonstrating her love for Jesus in this audacious way. In this sense, the fragrance of Christ represents her thankfulness for sins forgiven; Jesus allowed her to express her love by this act, knowing it was inspired by the Holy Spirit, as she put the Father's will above the rules of human convention. This biblical account thus symbolises the thankfulness of believers who, through the Holy Spirit, carry the fragrance of Christ, which brings life.

---

32 ¶ We can partake of His nature

Believers can become partakers of the nature of Christ, but may or may not manifest this. Christ was completely approachable, and everyone felt safe in His company. However, some believers have the effect of intimidating their fellow Christians, whilst others find themselves in awe of certain individuals. Christ did not intend this to be true of any of His followers because He wants all people to feel comfortable in their presence. It is the unredeemed old nature that regards other people as inferior, or as threatening. The apostle Peter explains that as we grow in our intimate knowledge of Christ we will have access to everything we need to live a godly life. According to His promise to us, we are able to escape the corrupting desires of the world, and become partakers of His divine nature. Peter urges believers not merely to be content that they have been saved through faith, but to aspire to building Christlike characteristics into their lives (see 2 Peter 1:3-8). Some bible versions have translated Peter's words as 'make every effort'. However, this does not suggest we can rely on our own strength to become godly. However, following this entreaty Peter adds the phrase 'by your faith', which immediately suggests the change will happen through dialogue with God, as we allow Him to point out the negative elements of our human nature that He wishes to overwrite with His own nature: 'Be imitators of God, as beloved children' (Ephesians 5:1). Believers are able to imitate God as they partake of His nature.

HOPE: DRIVING OUR DESTINY

A WORK OF THE HOLY SPIRIT

5

———

THE NATURE OF THE HOLY SPIRIT

33. He was involved in creation
34. He is God at work on earth
35. He is not abstract, but real
36. He incarnated Christ and raised Him from
    death
37. He is sensitive
38. He is the Spirit of truth
39. He communicated with the prophets
40. He is one with the Father and the Son

33 ¶ HE WAS INVOLVED IN CREATION

The Holy Spirit is first mentioned by name in the opening verses of the Bible: 'In the beginning God created the heavens and the earth. Now the earth was formless and empty, darkness was over the surface of the deep, and the Spirit of God was hovering over the waters' (Genesis 1:1-2 NIV). In fact, the Holy Spirit is the person of the Trinity who has always worked on the earth, right from the outset. In the continuing work of God, the Holy Spirit has endowed God's people with the resources required for creative activities that advance His kingdom on the earth. In one example, the Holy Spirit gave Bezalel the skills for building the tabernacle where God was to be worshipped by His people: 'The Lord told Moses, "I have called by name Bezalel, the son of Uri, the son of Hur, of the tribe of Judah. I have filled him with the Spirit of God in wisdom, in understanding, in knowledge, and in all kinds of craftsmanship, to make artistic designs for work in gold, in silver, and in bronze, and in the cutting of stones for settings, and in the carving of wood, that he may work in all kinds of craftsmanship"' (Exodus 31:1-5). The Holy Spirit was not only involved in the original creation of the earth, but He continues to impart creativity in the lives of believers.

34 ¶ He is God at work on earth

The Holy Spirit reveals God's work on earth. The apostle Paul was invited to explain about his God to the crowd at Athens, and this is what he said: 'The God who made the world and everything in it, since He is Lord of heaven and earth, does not dwell in temples constructed by human hands; nor is He served by human hands, as though He needed anything, because He Himself gives all creatures their life and breath and everything else. He made from one root every race of humanity to live on all the face of the earth, determining their appointed times and the boundaries of their habitation, to seek God, if they search for Him and find Him. Actually He is not far from each one of us; for in Him we live and move and exist…' (Acts 17:24-28). When Jesus spoke of His death and ascension back to the Father, He told the disciples: 'I tell you the truth, it is to your advantage that I go away; for if I do not go away, the Helper will not come to you; but if I go, I will send Him to you' (John 16:7 NASB). The Holy Spirit did indeed come to Christ's followers at Pentecost, and ever since, He has continued to work in the lives of believers, and non-believers. The God of heaven is revealed in the Holy Spirit. He is in creation, yet is also transcendent.

35 ¶ HE IS NOT ABSTRACT, BUT REAL

God is real. We know from church teaching that God constitutes a Trinity—Father, Son, and Holy Spirit. It is easily understood that God is a Father because He has a Son, Jesus. And it is self-evident that Jesus is God the Son, because He has a Father. However, for some people, God the Holy Spirit is an enigma. Some might say the Holy Spirit is the 'mystery person' of the Trinity.

Although the Holy Spirit is not often discussed this does not mean He is not real, or that He is merely an indefinable force. In fact He is a living personality with whom believers can have a relationship. As we are led by the Holy Spirit we become sensitised to His feelings and His desires.

John the Baptist described the moment Jesus' identity was revealed to him: John saw the Spirit come down from heaven in the form of a dove and remain on Jesus. He explained that he personally did not know Him, but God the Father, who instructed John to baptise with water, said, 'The man on whom you see the Spirit descending and remaining is He who will baptize with the Holy Spirit' (John 1:32-33). In Matthew's gospel, the three persons of the Trinity are disclosed together at this moment: 'After being baptized, Jesus came up immediately from the water; and behold, the heavens were opened, and he saw the Spirit of God descending as a dove and lighting on Him, and behold, a voice out of the heavens said, "This is My beloved Son, in whom I am well-pleased."' (Matthew 3:16-17 NASB). Until this point Jesus was waiting for the coming of the person of the Holy Spirit before being commissioned by the Father. This moment, therefore, represents the beginning of Jesus enacting the specific purpose of His incarnation. The Holy Spirit then led Jesus into the wilderness to be tempted by the devil. This leading of the Spirit was so that Jesus, as the last Adam, would be able to achieve what the first Adam had failed to do, because he capitulated to the devil. Thus, this desert experience constituted the starting point of Jesus' redemptive ministry. This illustrates that the Holy Spirit is not only real, but that He was intimately involved in the ministry of Christ, and thereafter He has instigated and led the ministry of believers.

---

36 ¶ He incarnated Christ and raised Him from death

The two most miraculous and powerful events relating to Christ's life were His immaculate conception and His resurrection from the dead. The birth of Jesus Christ took place in this way: 'When His mother Mary was pledged in marriage to Joseph, before they had come together, she was found to be with child by the Holy Spirit. Because her husband Joseph was a just man and unwilling to disgrace her in public, he planned to release her quietly. But as he pondered this, behold, an angel of the Lord appeared to him in a dream, saying, "Joseph, son of David, do not be afraid to take Mary as your wife; for that which has been conceived in her is by the Holy Spirit. And she will bear a son, and you are to call Him Jesus, for He will save His people from their sins." All this took place so that what was spoken by the Lord through the prophet might be fulfilled: "Behold, the virgin shall conceive and give birth to a son, and they shall call Him Emmanuel," which is translated "God is with us"' (Matthew 1:18-23 Mounce). This account from Matthew's gospel records the testimony of Joseph. The Holy Spirit initially spoke the promise through the prophet Isaiah, and about seven hundred years later He fulfilled the promise through the conception of Christ.

The angel Gabriel was sent to Nazareth in Galilee, to a virgin engaged to a man called Joseph. After greeting her he said: "Do not be afraid, Mary; for you have found favour with God. And behold, you will conceive in your womb and bear a son, and you shall name Him Jesus. He will be great and will be called the Son of the Most High; and the Lord God will give Him the throne of His father David; and He will reign over the house of Jacob forever, and His kingdom will have no end." Mary said to the angel, "How can this be, since I am a virgin?" The angel answered and said to her, "The Holy Spirit will come upon you, and the power of the Most High will overshadow you; and for that reason the Holy Child shall be called the Son of God" (Luke 1:30-35 NASB). This account from Luke's gospel is a record of the testimony of Mary.

The Holy Spirit also raised Christ to life in the resurrection: 'If Christ is in you, though the body is dead because of sin, yet the spirit is alive because of righteousness. But if the Spirit of Him who raised Jesus from the dead dwells in you, He who raised Christ Jesus from the dead will also give life to your mortal bodies through His Spirit who dwells in you' (Romans 8:10-11 NASB). Because of 'the fall', over the course of time our human bodies deteriorate and eventually die. Yet our awakened human spirit communes with the Holy Spirit in this life, and when our body eventually dies, we also will be given a new body: 'So will it be with the resurrection of the dead. The body that is sown is perishable, it is raised imperishable; it is sown in dishonour, it is raised in glory; it is sown in weakness, it is raised in power; it is sown a natural body, it is raised a spiritual body. If there is a natural body, there is also a spiritual body. So it is written: "The first man Adam became a living being"; the last Adam, a life-giving spirit. The spiritual did not come first, but the natural, and after that the spiritual. The first man was of the dust of the earth; the second man is of heaven. As was the earthly man, so are those who are of the earth; and as is the heavenly man, so also are those who are of heaven. And just as we have borne the image of the earthly man, so shall we bear the image of the heavenly man' (1 Corinthians 15:42-49 NIV). The Holy Spirit incarnated and resurrected Christ, and today He imparts resurrection life to believers.

---

37 ¶ HE IS SENSITIVE

The Spirit of God is sensitive. Because the Holy Spirit is the person of the Trinity who lives within believers, He is continuously aware of our emotional state, our thoughts and our attitudes. Jesus explains how the Trinity gives consideration to the Holy Spirit: 'Any sin and blasphemy shall be forgiven people, but blasphemy against the Spirit shall not be forgiven. Whoever speaks a word against the Son of Man, it shall be forgiven him; but whoever speaks against the Holy Spirit, it shall not be forgiven him, either in this age or in the age to come' (Matthew 12:31-32). There is no source of forgiveness other than through communion with the Holy Spirit, the Spirit of truth, thus whilst we remain under Satan's deception we are not able to experience forgiveness.

This is exemplified in the case of Judas Iscariot, who committed an appalling sin in betraying Christ. Afterwards he felt remorse, gave back the money he was paid for betraying Jesus, and then killed himself. He could have experienced forgiveness, even for this most terrible of sins. But Judas was deceived into trying to pay the price for his own sins, and he sentenced himself to the death penalty. Jesus reflects sadness over Judas in His prayer to His Father: 'While I was with them, I protected them in your name, which you have given me. I guarded them, and not one of them has been lost, except the son of destruction' (John 17:12 Mounce). When later God apprehended Saul, who became the apostle Paul, God demonstrated that a person can be redeemed regardless of the severity of their sins. Satan deceives people into trying to atone for their sin through their own efforts, whereas the Holy Spirit gives revelation, by grace, of the forgiveness which is already accomplished, through Christ's atonement for our sin.

Believers are also encouraged to be sensitive to the feelings of the Holy Spirit, and toward other believers: 'As God's chosen ones, holy and beloved, clothe yourselves with compassion, kindness, humility, meekness, and patience. Bear with one another and, if anyone has a complaint against another, forgive each other; just as the Lord has forgiven you, so you also must forgive. Above all, clothe yourselves with love, which binds everything together in perfect harmony. And let the peace of Christ rule in your hearts, to which indeed you were called in the one body. And be thankful' (Colossians 3:12-15 NRSV). The Holy Spirit lives within believers, and His job is to transform us, leading us away from our erroneous way of life and making us increasingly like Jesus. He requires our cooperation in order to do this. He is sensitive to how we are feeling and will not force us to change, but He will progressively transform our desires when we do not impede Him.

38 ¶ He is the Spirit of truth

In this world which is filled with lies, deceptions, fallacies and misrepresentations, the Holy Spirit speaks truth to us. Jesus told His disciples: 'I have many more things to say to you, but you cannot bear them now. But when He, the Spirit of truth, comes, He will guide you into all the truth; for He will not speak on His own initiative, but whatever He hears, He will speak; and He will disclose to you what is to come. He will glorify Me, for He will take of Mine and will disclose it to you' (John 16:12-15 NASB). Jesus taught many things, but in this discourse He makes it clear that there is more to come. The gospel accounts record much of what Jesus said whilst on earth, but in order to learn more from Him we need the Holy Spirit. Therefore, disciples of today are to continue to listen to the Holy Spirit; He will reveal the truth and not lead us away from the gospel. 'When the Advocate comes, whom I will send to you from the Father—the Spirit of truth, who goes out from the Father—He will testify about Me. And you also must testify, for you have been with Me from the beginning' (John 15:26-27 NIV). The Holy Spirit witnesses to the reality of Jesus and His true nature, and we may also be called to speak the truth about Jesus, and any other matter, as the Spirit of God prompts us.

39 ¶ He communicated with the prophets

The Spirit of God is the conduit between the heavenly realm and humanity: '...no prophecy ever came by the impulse of man, but men moved by the Holy Spirit spoke from God' (2 Peter 1:21 RSV). Whenever God speaks, His word remains in the world until such time as somebody engages with it and accepts it: 'So shall My word be that goes out from My mouth; it shall not return to Me empty, but it shall accomplish that which I purpose, and succeed in the thing for which I sent it' (Isaiah 55:11 NRSV). For example, by the time of Jesus' birth various prophecies had been formulated into a theology of a coming Messiah (Christ) and there was a real sense of expectancy (see king Herod's words in Matthew 2:4, Andrew's words in John 1:41 and the Samaritan woman's words in John 4:25). However, the significance of what God is saying is not necessarily understood, possibly not even by the person who prophesies. Paul told the crowd: 'The Holy Spirit spoke the truth to your ancestors when He said, through Isaiah the prophet, "Go to this people and say, 'You will hear but never understand; you will see but never perceive'"' (Acts 28:25-26 NIV). But because God has a purpose whenever He prompts the prophet to speak, it is wise to ask God for further revelation in order to gain understanding (see Matthew 13:34-36). Paul also encourages believers to seek the gift of prophecy: 'Pursue love, and earnestly desire the spiritual gifts, but especially that you may prophesy' (1 Corinthians 14:1).

When the Holy Spirit comes in power upon anyone there is a compulsion to speak the words He gives: 'Then Saul sent messengers to take David, but when they saw the company of the prophets prophesying, with Samuel standing and presiding over them, the Spirit of God came upon the messengers of Saul; and they also prophesied' (1 Samuel 19:20 NASB). This illustrates that God can speak prophetically through anybody, and also that the words spoken have an impact of some kind on all those who hear. In the time of the old covenant, for instance, the Holy Spirit spoke many things to the prophets in order to prepare the Jewish leaders to recognise the signs of the incarnation of Christ—the most important event of all time. However, when the time arrived, Satan deceived the chief priests and Pharisees, who chose to disregard the prophetic evidence which revealed the identity of Jesus as their Messiah. After Jesus had been rejected by the religious leaders, crucified, and had risen from the dead, He then appeared to two disciples on the road to Emmaus, and to the disciples in Jerusalem: 'But He said, "Why are you so agitated, and why are these doubts rising in your hearts? Look at my hands and feet; yes, it is I indeed. Touch me and see for yourselves; a ghost has no flesh and bones as you can see I have." And as He said this He showed them His hands and feet. Their joy was so great that they still could not believe it, and they stood there dumbfounded; so He said to them, "Have you anything here to eat?" And they offered Him a piece of grilled fish, which He took and ate before their eyes. Then He told them, "This is what I meant when I said, while I was still with you, that everything written about me in the Law of Moses, in the Prophets and in the Psalms has to be fulfilled". He then opened their minds to understand the scriptures' (Luke 24:38-45 JB). The Holy Spirit had already revealed the things concerning Christ to the prophets, centuries earlier.

---

40 ¶ HE IS ONE WITH THE FATHER AND THE SON

The Holy Spirit is part of the Godhead and, by definition, He is one with the Father and the Son. Scripture explains that, 'the Spirit searches all things, yes, the deep things of God. For what man knows the things of a man except the spirit of the man which is in him? Even so no one knows the things of God except the Spirit of God. Now we have received, not the spirit of the world, but the Spirit who is from God, that we might know the things that have been freely given to us by God' (1 Corinthians 2:10-12 NKJV). The three persons of the Trinity are together in perfect union, each having the same desires but enacting them in specific ways. Peter, for example, writing to believers who were scattered throughout the Roman world, describes them as those who have been chosen according to the foreknowledge of God the Father, through the sanctifying work of the Holy Spirit, for obedience to Jesus Christ, and made clean by His blood (see 1 Peter 1:2). Paul writes to the Ephesians and urges them to protect their unity, reminding them that all believers share a relationship with the Trinity: 'We are one body, we have one Spirit, and we are called to one glorious hope; one Lord, one faith, one baptism, one

God and Father of all who is over all, and through all, and in all' (Ephesians 4:4-6).

Jesus emphasised the undivided nature of the Trinity when He commissioned believers to take the gospel to the ends of the earth: 'All authority in heaven and on earth has been given to Me. Therefore go and make disciples of all nations, baptizing them in the name of the Father and of the Son and of the Holy Spirit' (Matthew 28:18-19 NIV). Christians of the first millennium had an appreciation of the Trinity which is less common in believers today. The prayers of these early believers, invoking the Trinity, reveal that they had an intimacy and awareness of God that suffused every element of their lives: 'The sacred Three, to save, to shield the hearth, the house, the household, this eve, this night, Oh! this eve, this night, and every night, each single night. Amen.' (Anon. from Carmina Gadelica, in David Adam ed., 1996. *The Wisdom of the Celts*. Lion Publishing, Singapore, p.31).

6

THE WORK OF THE HOLY SPIRIT

41. The Holy Spirit shows us our deceptions
42. The Holy Spirit corrects us
43. The Holy Spirit guides our prayers
44. The Holy Spirit is our Paraclete
45. The Holy Spirit teaches us all things
46. The Holy Spirit reminds us of everything Jesus said
47. The Holy Spirit gives us liberty
48. The Holy Spirit tells us things yet to come

41 ¶ THE HOLY SPIRIT SHOWS US OUR DECEPTIONS

The Spirit of God reveals the lies and falsehoods we believe. The book of Genesis tells us that Adam and Eve had a close relationship with God and everything was provided for them. The serpent initiated a conversation with Eve and suggested that God might not have meant what He said. After she had explained that God warned them not to eat from one of the trees, and His reasons, that is to say, that God did not want them to die, the serpent retorted 'You surely will not die. For God knows that in the day you eat from it your eyes will be opened, and you will be like God, knowing good and evil' (Genesis 3:4-5). Here, Satan is telling Eve that God is a liar, that He is stopping Adam and Eve from becoming something better, that He does not want them to know the things He knows, and that His motives are selfish. Christians are all too familiar with the 'sinful effects of the fall', attributed to Adam and Eve's eating of the 'apple'. But most terrible was that they swallowed the lies of Satan, and started believing that God is not to be trusted, that He does not want our best, that He wants us subjugated to Him. It is not surprising that Adam and Eve hid behind a tree from the presence of God—the lies they now believed made them afraid of Him. Please note that God did not hide Himself from them. God's next act was to help Adam and Eve with the awkward situation in which they found themselves, providing them with clothing to put on. And even in this moment, God pledged the incarnation of Jesus, which was specifically targeted at undoing humankind's fateful error. He says to the serpent: 'I will put enmity between you and the woman, and between your seed and her Seed; He shall bruise your head, and you shall bruise His heel' (Genesis 3:15 NKJV). Jesus, born of a woman, is the 'Seed' referred to here. But tragically, it seems the deception of Satan entered the DNA of humankind, so that generation after generation have found it difficult to believe that God is good and kind. Unable to risk trusting God, people try to appease their passions with soulish pleasures, and to escape their sense of emptiness by imagining themselves to be something special. The sin of Adam and Eve is often called 'original sin', and it is common to humanity from birth. For instance, when young toddlers sense they are being accused of misbehaviour by an adult, they instinctively say 'it wasn't me'—even though it was. In this sense, 'original sin' might be better called 'original deception', since we are unaware that God created us to be the object of His love. This is the reason we need to be born again, which marks the start of our awareness that He has made us perfect, and of our progressively living in this reality. Jesus tells those who believed in Him that they can be freed from deception: 'If you continue in my word, you are truly my disciples, and you will know the truth, and the truth will make you free' (John 8:31-32).

The Holy Spirit works to bring non-believers to the realisation of their need for God. Jesus explains how the Holy Spirit will operate once He Himself has returned to the Father: 'When the Holy Spirit comes He will convict the world in respect of sin and righteousness and judgment; in respect of sin, because they do not believe in Me; and in respect of righteousness, because I go to the Father and you no longer see Me; and in respect of judgment, because the ruler of this world has been judged' (John 16:8-11). The Holy Spirit works uniquely with each person, according to their experiences of life, and the deceptions that drive them. He also makes people feel uncomfortable with their guilt. Not believing in Jesus is the sin; 'believing' is the antidote that the Holy Spirit provides. In terms of righteousness, when a person becomes aware of their wrongdoing, and turns to God, righteousness is credited to them as a consequence of their faith. In respect of judgment, God does not rule by fear, but instead the Holy Spirit reveals the reality of the destructive intentions of Satan, as He progressively removes our deceptions. The bible says that: 'The fear of the Lord is the beginning of wisdom' (Psalm 111:10) which refers to the initial response of the unrenewed mind when becoming aware of God. When a believer responds to the prompting of God, however, this fear is displaced by His love. Although we 'work out our salvation with fear and trembling' (Philippians 2:12), this indicates the process of entering into God's rest where 'there is no fear in love; but perfect love drives out fear, because fear involves punishment, therefore the one who fears is not perfected in love' (1 John 4:18). This scripture points out the root of human fear: it was the devil's deception of Adam and Eve in the Garden of Eden which led them to think God had stopped loving them and wanted to punish them, motivating them to hide from Him.

42 ¶ The Holy Spirit corrects us

The Holy Spirit has the task of guiding us to live our lives in a way that is pleasing to God. 'After removing Saul, God made David the king of Israel. God testified about him: "I have found David, the son of Jesse, who is a man after My own heart; he will do everything I want him to do"' (Acts 13:22). For the remainder of his life, David experienced God's discipline and intimacy, as from a loving parent. David wrote Psalm 139, which is an encouragement for all future generations who will experience the work of the Holy Spirit in their lives. He is deeply thankful to live in the presence of God: 'Lord, You have searched me and know me. You know when I sit down and when I get up; You understand my thoughts from afar. You watch my going out and my lying down; You see all my ways. Before I utter a word You know exactly what I will say. You are all around me, and Your hand is upon me. All this is amazing and beyond my understanding. Wherever I am Your Spirit is with me. If I ascend to the heavens You are there; if I lie down in the depths You are there. Even in the remotest parts of the earth Your hand will guide me, Your right hand will hold me' (see Psalm 139:1-10). David also knew God's heart, and desired to please Him. Therefore he asked Him to remove any hindrance to their intimacy: 'Search me, God, and know my heart; test me and know my anxious thoughts. See if there is any

offensive way in me, and lead me in the way everlasting'
(Psalm 139:23-24 NIV).

God told the prophet Jonah to go to the city of
Nineveh and warn the people to repent. But Jonah did
not agree that God should give them a chance to repent,
so he decided to flee to Tarshish instead, away from the
presence of the Lord. He boarded a ship, but on the
voyage a huge storm arose. Jonah knew this was because
of his disobedience, so he told the crew to throw him
overboard and the sea became calm. The Lord
appointed a great sea creature to swallow Jonah, and
inside its stomach Jonah prayed for help. Then the Lord
commanded the sea creature to vomit up Jonah onto dry
land, and He again told him to go to Nineveh. On
hearing Jonah's message the Ninevites repented, but
Jonah was furious because he wanted them punished. So
he prayed to the Lord, saying, 'This is exactly what I
thought would happen when I was still at home. This is
why I fled to Tarshish, to avoid this very thing, because I
know You are gracious and merciful, slow to anger and
always kind, and You show pity rather than inflicting
punishment. So, please let me die! (see Jonah 4:1-3). But
God's response was to teach Jonah to see those people as
He sees them, using a plant which sprang up overnight
and then withered away, as an illustration. The Lord
explained to Jonah, 'You had compassion on the plant
even though you did not plant it or nurture it—it just
sprung up and shrivelled overnight. Should I then not
have compassion on Nineveh, where more than 120,000

people live, who do not know the difference between their right and left hand, not to mention all the animals?' (see Jonah 4:10-11). God disciplined Jonah in order to teach him love.

The Holy Spirit, who is living within God's children today, has the task of urging us to allow Him to remove our habits, attitudes, and beliefs which are in conflict with the values and truth of God.

The writers of Hebrews point out that Jesus was relentlessly provoked to induce Him to sin. This would have ruined His mission had He capitulated, but He resisted even though He was subjected to violence and crucifixion. By comparison, believers suffer far less opposition and temptation. Yet at those times when we do have to face hardship we can regard this as divine discipline, thereby understanding that God works even through our suffering to achieve a higher purpose. We are encouraged neither to be cavalier about it, nor to be crushed by it, because discipline is an intrinsic element of the parent-child relationship. However, in the case of God, He never disciplines us for any negative reason— He is never in a bad mood, for example. On the contrary, His only motive is to develop the character of His children: 'We have all had human fathers who disciplined us and we respected them for it. How much more should we submit to the Father of spirits and live! They disciplined us for a short time as it suited them, but God disciplines us for our benefit, so we will share His holy character. Discipline always seems unpleasant at the time, but later it produces righteousness and peace' (see Hebrews 12:4-11). In actual fact, not everyone had a human father who disciplined them well. However, God handles each of His children in a way that is perfect for them, taking into consideration all the experiences they have faced in life.

---

43 ¶ THE HOLY SPIRIT GUIDES OUR PRAYERS

Jesus taught us that we should pray, and the Holy Spirit shows us how. God could do everything without us, but instead He has chosen to do things through us. This choice goes right back to the beginnings of the human race, when God assigned to Adam and Eve dominion and stewardship of the earth—which was made for the benefit of humankind. Adam and Eve were originally tasked with administrating God's will on earth, but they were foolishly tricked into relinquishing their realm of jurisdiction to Satan. As a result, the earth became a place of suffering, and humankind then became the perpetrators, and the victims, of wrongdoing. More than once God considered eliminating the human race and starting again, but ultimately through Jesus' work, human beings can be recreated as children of God. And God wants His children to be involved with His affairs on earth, therefore He wants us to be aligned with the way He feels about situations. Naturally, when we are troubled by suffering in our own lives, or in the lives of those we care about, we cry out to God in prayer. But God knows all things, and He cares about everything that happens on the earth. And He alone understands what is the best solution in every situation: 'The Spirit helps our weakness; for we do not know how to pray as we should, but the Spirit Himself intercedes for us with groanings too deep for words; and He who searches the heart knows what the desire of the Spirit is, because He intercedes for the saints according to the will of God' (Romans 8:26-27). It is His desire that we join Him in His ongoing work on the earth by praying, guided by the Holy Spirit. Because God has given the earth to humankind, He waits for an invitation to act: this is what prayer actually is—God does not act sovereignly on earth. Somewhere there are people praying in the background, and God has always had people after His own heart who were praying in alignment with His will. There are examples of such people in both old and new covenant contexts. One Old Testament example was Daniel, a young man who was taken into captivity by the Babylonians. He loved God and prayed faithfully three times every day, even when he knew he would be thrown into the lion's den for doing so (see Daniel 6). In due time his prayers were instrumental in the captive Jews returning to their homeland. In Luke's gospel we read of an eighty-four year old woman, Anna, who prayed and fasted in the temple, day and night. The moment the eight-day-old baby Jesus was brought to the temple, she came up and gave thanks to God and spoke about the child to all who were looking for the redemption of Jerusalem (Luke 2:38). As we allow the Holy Spirit to guide our prayer life, God will increasingly conform our desires to His.

---

44 ¶ The Holy Spirit is our Paraclete

When Jesus announces to the disciples that He is going back to the Father, He promises them that they will be given another companion. In the Greek text, the word He used is 'Paraclete' meaning someone who will always stand by us throughout life. The Holy Spirit will not go away from us, but He will stick with us to the end, and help us to follow Christ. As He explained to His disciples, 'I will ask the Father, and He will give you another advocate to help you, and to be with you forever—the Spirit of truth. The world cannot receive Him because it neither sees Him nor knows Him. But you know Him, because He lives with you, and will be in you' (John 14:16-17). Christ promises that the Holy Spirit will also act as our legal advocate: 'Whenever they bring you before the synagogues, rulers and authorities, do not worry about your defence or what you should say, for the Holy Spirit will teach you at that very moment exactly what to say' (Luke 12:11-12).

When the disciples were arrested and brought before the High Priest for questioning, the Holy Spirit gave Peter such eloquence and wisdom that he was able to confound the accusers. At the same time he was given the boldness to admonish the religious leaders for rejecting Jesus: 'You ask by what power or in what name this man was healed. Well, this man stands before you healed by the name of Jesus Christ of Nazareth, whom you crucified but whom God raised from the dead. Jesus is the stone you builders rejected, and He has become the cornerstone, and salvation is found in no one else, for there is no other name under heaven given to humankind by which we must be saved.' The religious leaders were unable to deny that a miracle had occurred, but they were also astonished to see that these uneducated men, who had been with Jesus, clearly carried authority and had the ability to present a theological argument (see Acts 4:8-21).

The Holy Spirit gives guidance and wisdom to believers. The following scripture shows that the elders of the early church discussed, and sought the Holy Spirit together before they decided what advice they would give to the new gentile believers: 'It seemed good to the Holy Spirit and to us not to place on you any greater burden than these essentials...' (see Acts 15:28-29). The scriptures show the Holy Spirit went on to address unhelpful practices within new believers' cultures, steering them toward life and godliness. Whenever we take the trouble to seek Him, the Holy Spirit will advise us according to our best interests, taking into account the cultural influences of our own day. He desires to be involved in everything believers do.

---

45 ¶ THE HOLY SPIRIT TEACHES US ALL THINGS

The apostle John wrote a letter to believers because false teachers were causing confusion. He points out that the Holy Spirit within us is our only true teacher, and we therefore need to continually refer back to Him: 'You have an anointing from the Holy One, and all of you know the truth. I am not writing to you because you do not know the truth, but because you do know it, and because no lie comes from the truth'. 'The anointing you received from Him abides in you, and you do not need anyone to teach you because His anointing teaches you about everything and is true, and is not a lie' (1 John 2:20-21 & 27). Although this scripture tells believers they do not need anyone to teach them, we also know that the early church did teach new believers. Yet even when we listen to teaching in the church, it is the Holy Spirit who will reveal the things of God, through our spirit, to our mind. If we submit to Him rather than to man, He will arbitrate between what is good for us to hear and that which is unhelpful.

The Book of Nehemiah records the prayers of thanks that were offered when the people of Israel finished rebuilding the ruined city walls of Jerusalem. Their prayer recalls His kindness to them during the forty years when they walked through the wilderness. We see that even then, God taught His people through the Holy Spirit: 'The pillar of cloud led them by day, and the pillar of fire guided them by night. You gave Your good Spirit to instruct them. You gave them Your manna to eat and water to drink' (Nehemiah 9:19-20). Long before Christ's incarnation the Holy Spirit was a guide and teacher to God's people.

---

46 ¶ The Holy Spirit reminds us of everything Jesus said

The Pharisees studied the scriptures diligently and thus were able to quote the texts at will. They put in a great deal of effort and they believed they had earned, and deserved, the respect of others. Some may have looked down on people who were less educated, but they also took offence that Jesus had more wisdom than they did: 'On the Sabbath day Jesus began to teach in the synagogue, and many who heard Him were astounded. "Where did this man get these things?" they asked. "What is this wisdom that has been given Him? How are these powerful works happening through His hands? Surely, this is the carpenter, the son of Mary and the brother of Jacob, Joseph, Judas and Simon? Are not His sisters here with us?" And they took offence at Him' (Mark 6:2-3). After the Holy Spirit came upon the disciples at Pentecost, He empowered those common men to quote appropriate scripture, to speak about Jesus, and to relate His teachings with authority. The disciples were commissioned by Jesus to be His witnesses because they had been with Him from the beginning. Therefore it was vital that they accurately remember everything He said and did. Jesus explained to them that after He had returned to the Father, He would send them the Holy Spirit in Jesus' place, and He would teach the disciples all things, and remind them of everything Jesus had said (see John 14:25-26). Thus, Christ's teaching would not merely be entrusted to the fragility of human memory, but each time a believer was to speak on Christ's behalf the Holy Spirit would give the right words. The Holy Spirit would always glorify Christ, because everything He reveals will have come from Christ (see John 16:14-15). In this way God is pleased to exclude from His kingdom all hierarchy based on academic ability. He deliberately chose the foolish things of the world in order to shame the wise; He also chose the weak things of the world to shame the strong, and He chose the insignificant and despised, regarded as nothing, to negate the things that are, so no one can boast in His presence (see 1 Corinthians 1:27-29). Even the Apostle Paul, who was a highly educated Pharisee, resolved not to use his own hard-won theological knowledge, as he explained: It was the wisdom of God that the world's wisdom did not bring people to know Him. Rather, God is pleased to save whoever believes through the foolishness of the message of the cross. (see 1 Corinthians 1:20-25). We can rely on the Holy Spirit to bring to mind the things Jesus said, at the relevant time.

---

47 ¶ THE HOLY SPIRIT GIVES US LIBERTY

Jesus was anointed by the Holy Spirit to liberate people from the oppression of Satan. After Jesus returned from the wilderness, where He had been subjected to the devil's temptations, He was empowered by the Holy Spirit in a new way. He went in to the synagogue in His home town of Nazareth on the sabbath day, and stood up to read. The scroll of the prophet Isaiah was handed to Him, and from this He read out: 'The Spirit of the Lord is upon me, because He has anointed me to bring good news to the poor. He has sent me to proclaim release to the captives and recovery of sight to the blind, to let the oppressed go free, to proclaim the year of the Lord's favour.' He gave back the scroll, sat down, then explained 'Today, this scripture has been fulfilled in your hearing'. Through this prophecy Isaiah described Jesus' ministry (see Luke 4:16-21). There is no greater satisfaction than the fullness of life that Christ's followers can access when they live in freedom in the Spirit: 'I have come that they may have life, and have it to the full' (John 10:10 NIV).

Non-believers might consider liberty to be synonymous with personal sovereignty, thus they may assume believers give up their liberty when they surrender their lives to Christ. But in fact, believers are liberated from the oppression of Satan, in addition to retaining their sovereignty: 'The Lord is the Spirit, and where the Spirit of the Lord is, there is liberty' (2 Corinthians 3:17).

---

48 ¶ THE HOLY SPIRIT TELLS US THINGS YET TO COME

The Holy Spirit spoke at different times and in various ways to the prophets of the old covenant (see Hebrews 1:1). So, even before the incarnation of Jesus, the Holy Spirit revealed to God's friends many things that were to take place in the future, the most wonderful of which were things concerning the coming Messiah: 'The Lord Himself will give you a sign: Behold, a virgin will be with child and bear a son, and she will call His name Immanuel' (see Isaiah 7:14). Today the Holy Spirit speaks to us and He will also reveal what is to come—for the sake of our prayers, our preparedness, and our protection. Jesus told His followers that the Holy Spirit 'will tell you what is yet to come' (John 16:13). There are several passages in the bible which refer to events at the end of the age, such as Daniel 9, and Matthew 24 where the disciples asked Christ what would happen in the future. John also had visions about the time of the end, which are recorded in the book of Revelation. These things remain mysteries and yet we will have them revealed to us personally, by the Holy Spirit, at the appropriate time. Paul wrote to the church at Thessalonica about the end times, and the return of Christ, however, Paul said he did not need to write regarding times and dates. He reminded them that the day of the Lord would come like a thief in the night, when people are complacent, thinking there is peace and security, destruction will suddenly come, like a pregnant woman's labour pains, which cannot be avoided. But, he tells them believers will not be taken by surprise by events, since we are not in spiritual darkness (see 1 Thessalonians 5:1-4). Therefore we do not need to be anxious about these things but rather, as Paul advises, 'be very aware of how you live, not unwisely, but as wise people, make the most of every opportunity because the times are evil. Do not be foolish, but understand what the will of the Lord is' (Ephesians 5:15-17). The Holy Spirit does not want believers to be afraid about things that may happen in the future, but wants us to rest in the knowledge that He is never taken unawares, therefore we can simply trust Him.

OUR RELATIONSHIP WITH THE HOLY SPIRIT

49. We are sons of God as we are led by the Holy Spirit
50. We are transitioning into the character of Christ
51. We receive the Holy Spirit as a pledge of our inheritance
52. We grieve the Holy Spirit when we ignore Him
53. We are marked with the seal of ownership
54. We have a sense of adoption from the Holy Spirit
55. We abound in hope and power by the Holy Spirit
56. We are temples for the Holy Spirit

49 ¶ We are sons of God as we are led by the Holy Spirit

The desire of God is that believers are led by the Holy Spirit. At the creation of man described in Genesis, after man had been formed from the dust of the earth, God breathed His spirit (Greek: pneuma) into man, and he became alive (see Genesis 2:7). Thus the created human spirit is the life-sustaining part of human beings that was initially formed in us by God's Spirit, and now constitutes our human spirit. Indeed, the life of all things is sustained by His powerful Word, by God, who is spiritual (see John 1:1, John 4:24, Hebrews 1:3). Christ awakens our consciousness to our human spirit when we receive spiritual revelation (see Revelation 3:2). This experience resonates with us because our human spirit is already aware of Him, but in the human soul our sense of Him is dormant, and needs to be awakened.

The existence of two trees in the Garden of Eden illustrates how we can live by the influence of the spirit, or the soul. When Adam and Eve both ate the fruit from the tree of the knowledge of good-and-evil, their pure sense of God was lost, and instead they became conscious of, and deceived by, Satan's version of the law. As the mind (soul) focuses on any moral law, we either feel shame as we become aware of our shortcomings, or we feel proud and self-righteous if we think we are fulfilling that law. Yet when we eat from the tree of life (spirit) we transcend law, no longer subject to either the self-loathing or the pride. Then

Christ enables us to rest from our self-effort, because revelation is given and received purely by grace, and God puts His will within us and writes it on our hearts (see Jeremiah 31:33).

It is the will of the Father that believers are led by the Holy Spirit, and this is what defines them as Sons of God (see Romans 8:14). We are all capable of being led by the soul, or the Spirit, but Paul exhorts us to be spiritual so that our souls are then subject to the leading of the Holy Spirit. He explains that if believers walk by the Spirit they will not be driven to gratify the desires of the flesh. This is because the desires of the flesh are contrary to the Spirit, and the Spirit longs for what is contrary to the flesh. These are in conflict with each other, thwarting our best intentions. However, if we are led by the Spirit we do not come under the rules of the Law. Clearly, the flesh is drawn towards sexual immorality, lewdness, licentiousness, idolatry, drug abuse, fighting, arguing, malice, rage, selfish ambition, superiority, factions, spitefulness, drunkenness, vandalism and so on. These behaviours are completely out of keeping with the kingdom of God. However, the fruit of the Spirit is love, joy, peace, forbearance, kindness, generosity, faithfulness, gentleness and self-control, and of course, there are no laws that forbid those things! Since Christ Jesus has crucified the flesh with its passions and desires we can live by the Spirit, and stay in step with the Spirit (see Galatians 5:16-25). Hence, when believers are led by the Spirit, the Law is an irrelevance because the Holy Spirit will never contravene the will of the Father.

---

50 ¶ WE ARE TRANSITIONING INTO THE CHARACTER OF CHRIST

The Holy Spirit desires that believers develop the character of Christ, as He nurtures their spiritual identity. Human beings are born with the nature of Adam and Eve after the fall, but the Holy Spirit causes believers' spiritual identity to gradually emerge: 'Flesh gives birth to flesh, but the Spirit gives birth to spirit' (John 3:6 NIV). As our spiritual identity becomes increasingly ascendant over our flesh, the Holy Spirit is able to change our character. Paul writes to encourage the believers in Rome: 'Make sure your love is genuine; reject everything evil, but embrace what is good; care for one another with brotherly love, and go out of your way to honour one another. Stay passionate in your faith, be ardent in spirit, serving the Lord. Rejoice in hope, be patient in suffering, persevere in prayer. Support your fellow believers who are in need and extend kindness to strangers. If anyone treats you badly, make sure you bless them, but never curse them. Rejoice with those who rejoice, weep with those who weep. Live in harmony with one another; do not be arrogant, but keep company with the lowly, and do not think you are doing them a favour' (Romans 12:9-16). These behaviours exemplify the character of Christ, and become joyful for the believer when they spring from a character that has been set free from self-interest and self-importance, instead displaying the love of Christ.

A major characteristic of Jesus was humility, and He gave His disciples a memorable demonstration of humility when He washed their feet. Afterwards He explained to them, 'I hope you realise what I have just done to you. You call Me Teacher and Lord, and of course that is correct. Now, since I have washed your feet as Lord and Teacher, you should wash one another's feet because I was giving you a model to follow' (see John 13:12-15). He desires believers to embrace humility, by deliberately surrendering their pride. The apostle Paul applies this principle not only to our deeds, but also to our attitude of mind, urging us to look to Jesus as our perfect example: 'Do not be selfish or conceited, but have humility of mind treating other people as more important than yourselves; do not look out just for your self, but also look out for the wellbeing of others. Have the same attitude as Christ Jesus, who existed in the form of God yet did not consider equality with God something to be held on to but emptied Himself, taking the form, and being born, in the likeness of a human being. And as a human being He humbled Himself, becoming submissive even to death on a cross' (Philippians 2:3-8). Although pride will remain an ever-present element of our humanity, whenever God makes us aware of it and its ugly nature, we can then purposely submit our pride to God: 'Humble yourselves in the presence of the Lord, and He will exalt you' (James 4:10). Peter advises believers to make a decision to adopt a humble attitude, using the phrase 'clothe yourselves with humility toward one another'. This suggests that humility is not a virtue imparted to us by God, but a choice that is within our control. Peter goes on to explain that God opposes the proud but gives grace to the humble. Therefore, as we imitate Christ by surrendering our human pretensions to God, not only do we gain access to heavenly resources, but also He is able to gain access to our unredeemed beliefs and affections (see 1 Peter 5:5-6). God initiates the entire process of believers becoming like Christ: 'By grace you have been saved through faith; and this was not something you had a hand in because it was a gift from God. It was not based on human works, so that nobody could take credit for it' (Ephesians 2:8-9). Believers are gradually being conformed to the character of Christ by the Spirit of God.

---

51 ¶ We receive the Holy Spirit as a pledge of our inheritance

The Holy Spirit residing in us gives assurance of everything God has promised Christ's followers, both now and in the future: 'When you believed in Christ you were marked with the seal of the Holy Spirit who is the guarantee of the inheritance He promised us, and that God will redeem us as His own people' (Ephesians 1:13-14). Once someone is born again as a child of God they begin to benefit from this spiritual inheritance. Because the Father has rescued believers from the powers of darkness and brought them into the kingdom of Jesus, this qualifies them to receive the same inheritance in heaven that is already enjoyed by the people of faith who are forerunners of all believers (see Colossians 1:12-13). In fact, the Holy Spirit Himself is a gift from Father God to believers, and He helps us to persevere throughout our lifetime, so that we will ultimately inherit all that God has prepared for us. Thus, whenever life becomes difficult the Holy Spirit will remind us that our true treasure is in heaven. Then after our bodies die we shall gain an eternal inheritance, as Peter points out: All those who are born again through Christ's resurrection shall obtain an inheritance which is reserved in heaven, beyond the reach of decay, corruption and depreciation' (see 1 Peter 1:3-5). Our spiritual inheritance is kept secure in heaven where it cannot be stolen or destroyed.

52 ¶ WE GRIEVE THE HOLY SPIRIT WHEN WE IGNORE HIM

The Holy Spirit lives in us, and His purpose is to lead us out of our soulish identity, where our ego habitually compares itself with other people; and away from the ungodly behaviours which result from the lies we believe. He will teach us, prompt us and provoke us, but He will not implement change until we are ready. He longs for our cooperation: 'Whoever wishes to be a friend of the world makes himself an enemy of God. Or do you think scripture has no meaning when it tells us that the Spirit He has caused to dwell in us jealously yearns for us?' (James 4:4-5). James was not quoting one specific scripture here, but rather, referring to the general concept of God's jealousy for His people, which is repeatedly stated in the Old Testament. When we ignore the Holy Spirit's prompting He is saddened but He will nevertheless continue His attempts to sanctify us, either by speaking directly to us, or through another believer, or through our circumstances. Paul writes to the Ephesians, pointing out the behaviours which distress the Holy Spirit: 'Stop wearing a mask but be truthful with one another; do not let your anger spill over into sin and deal with it at the first opportunity so the devil will not get a chance to make you bitter. Do not steal but work hard and do what is good with your own hands, then you will have something to contribute. Do not use foul language, but use your mouth to encourage and bless others. Do not grieve the Holy Spirit of God, by whom you were sealed for the day of redemption. Expel all bitterness, rage, vengeance, fighting and slander from your life, as well as all malice' (see Ephesians 4:25-31). This is not a call to make more effort to control our bad behaviours, but rather to acknowledge them, and then surrender them to God. Whenever we grieve the Holy Spirit we lose our sense of peace and joy, and this motivates us to seek God, who is then able to transform our heart and mind.

---

53 ¶ WE ARE MARKED WITH THE SEAL OF OWNERSHIP

In Christ we are God's possession, sealed by the Holy Spirit; yet at the same time, we are free: 'Whoever was called in the Lord whilst a slave is the Lord's freedman; likewise whoever was called whilst free is Christ's slave' (1 Corinthians 7:22). We experience liberty because there is no loss of decision-making capability or sovereignty, but nevertheless we are slaves to Him because our hearts have been changed, and serving Him brings us joy. Rather than having our will overruled, in Christ we discover who we truly are, and our will finds the object of its desire. Unlike a slave, we also discover we have honour and an eternal inheritance, beyond anything the world could ever give: 'Christ has anointed us, set His seal of ownership on us, and put His Spirit in our hearts as a deposit, guaranteeing what is to come' (2 Corinthians 1:21-22). Paul wrote to the Ephesians, 'Slaves, obey your earthly masters with fear and trembling, with sincerity of heart, as though obeying Christ. And not only while you are watched, to please people, but as slaves of Christ doing the will of God from the heart' (Ephesians 6:5-6).

In centuries past, this scripture has been used as an argument to support the continuation of human slavery. Yet William Wilberforce and the Clapham Sect understood the mind of Christ on this matter. They recognised this teaching was only addressed to a community of people who were powerless to do anything about the structure of their society, and therefore unable to advocate the abolition of slavery. Wilberforce, however, successfully achieved an end to the slave trade, despite much opposition. For believers today, more than two hundred years later, it is important to understand that the word of God is living and active, thus the Holy Spirit is revealing new and relevant understanding of scripture that can change our world at an individual and a systemic level. Now, marked as owned by God, believers enjoy a sense of belonging, as well as engagement with His will.

---

54 ¶ WE HAVE A SENSE OF ADOPTION FROM THE HOLY SPIRIT

Paul reminded the believers in Rome, 'You did not receive a spirit of slavery to lead you back into fear of a harsh master. Instead you received the Spirit of adoption, and through Him we cry out "Abba! Father!" The Spirit Himself bears witness with our spirit that we are now, in fact, children of God' (Romans 8:15-16). Here Paul contrasts the idea of a demanding, faultfinding deity who incites fear, and God the Father who tenderly wins the trust of His children.

Producing children is not the same as parenting, and many people have walked away from their families to be with a different partner. If anyone thinks adoption is a lesser form of parenthood they are mistaken, because in one sense, true fatherhood is by adoption. Thus, when a parent takes their new baby into their arms for the first time and looks into its face, and falls in love with the baby, they then have adopted it with their heart. This is what God intended to happen. And this is the way Father God adopts us, with the promise that He will never leave us or forsake us: 'Before the creation of the world God loved us, and chose to set us apart for Himself. He marked us out for adoption as His own, through Jesus Christ. This was His idea, and it makes Him joyful' (see Ephesians 1:4-6). When the Holy Spirit brings to our awareness the fact that Father God has deliberately chosen to adopt us, any feelings we may have of being alone, aimless or insignificant are displaced by a deep sense of security.

---

55 ¶ We abound in hope and power by the Holy Spirit

In our modern context the word hope is used to indicate wishfulness with an element of uncertainty, but in the New Testament context, hope indicates a certainty that is set in the future, confirmed in the believer by the Holy Spirit. Paul explains that not only are Jews and Gentiles now included in God's family, but that God expressed His intention to remove the barrier between them long ago, through the coming of Christ, as Isaiah writes: 'The root of Jesse will come, the One who rises to rule the Gentiles; in Him will the Gentiles hope'. May the God of hope fill you with all joy and peace as you trust Him, so you abound in hope by the power of the Holy Spirit (Romans 15:12-14). At one time, the promises of God were seen as exclusively for the Jewish people, but now the gentiles are irrefutably included. It is this God-given hope that sustains us through the difficult times in life, because it keeps our focus on eternity.

God also strengthens us with His Spirit. Paul prays, asking that, from the riches of His glory, God would strengthen believers in their inner being with the power of the Holy Spirit (see Ephesians 3:16). It is the power of the Holy Spirit that enables us to fulfil the specific destiny God has ordained for us, when often we are unable to do so through our natural abilities. Paul was aware of the futility of his human efforts and knowledge, particularly as a result of his experience on the road to Damascus, but he was confident in the power of God's Spirit, stating: 'I can do all things through the One who strengthens me' (Philippians 4:13 Mounce). The Holy Spirit gave Paul abundant hope and power from the heavenly realm.

56 ¶ WE ARE TEMPLES FOR THE HOLY SPIRIT

God does not live in buildings made by human hands, but within the believer: 'Do you not know that you are a temple of God and that the Spirit of God dwells in you?' (1 Corinthians 3:16). Paul was encouraging the believers in Corinth to regard their bodies as holy at a time when visiting prostitutes was common practice within their society: 'Everything is lawful for me, but not everything is helpful. Everything is lawful for me, but I will not be overpowered by anything. Food is for the stomach and the stomach is for food, but God will do away with both of them. But the body is not for sexual immorality, but for the Lord, and the Lord is for the body. God has not only raised the Lord, but will also raise us up by His power. Do you not know that your bodies are members of Christ? Shall I take the members of Christ and make them members of a prostitute? Certainly not! Whoever joins himself to a prostitute is one body with her, since, "the two become one flesh." But he who joins himself to the Lord is one spirit with Him. Flee sexual immorality. Most sin is committed outside the body, but with sexual immorality you sin against your own body. Do not forget your body is a temple of the Holy Spirit who is in you as a gift from God, and you are not your own' (1 Corinthians 6:12-19). This scripture has often been used to give guidelines on sexual behaviour. However, it is God's intention that believers have integrity in their sexuality, rather than following prescriptive instructions. In contrast, the devil seeks to undermine our sexual wholeness: 'The thief comes only to steal and kill and destroy; I came that they may have life, and have it abundantly' (John 10:10). In addition, whilst Paul is advising the believers on their behaviour, he is not suggesting we should try to impose the morality of the Kingdom of God on society at large: 'What business is it of mine to judge those outside the church? Are you not to judge those inside?' (1 Corinthians 5:12). The task of believers is to bring the gospel to those who do not know Christ, then subsequently to allow the Holy Spirit to do His work of sanctification, as He sees fit.

The Corinthian believers were also living in the midst of a society that practised idol worship, and Paul gave them some advice: There is no compatibility between Christ and the devil and a believer has nothing in common with an unbeliever. Likewise the temple of God has no compatibility with idols, and we are the temple of the living God, as He said, 'I will dwell in them and walk with them. I will be their God and they will be My people. So come out from their midst and be separate, and touch nothing unclean' (2 Corinthians 6:15-17). Paul was not suggesting that believers physically separate themselves from other people, otherwise they would cease to be salt and light for the world (see Matthew 5:13-16). In fact, Paul advises believers to be wise and courteous whenever they did accept an invitation to eat at an unbeliever's home: 'If an unbeliever invites you to a meal and you decide to go, eat whatever is set before you, and do not ask any questions based on conscience' (1 Corinthians 10:27). Paul merely urges them to abstain from idol worship, and all other evil practices. Thus, he was recommending a different behaviour paradigm—living by the Spirit in the midst of their society. Paul wanted believers always to remember that they are temples for the Holy Spirit.

8

OUR IDENTITY IN THE HOLY SPIRIT

57. We can facilitate or quench the Holy Spirit
58. We belong to one spiritual family
59. We embody the joy and peace of the Holy Spirit
60. We are all part of one royal priesthood
61. We are a new order of people
62. We are entrusted with spiritual gifts
63. We continue His work
64. We participate in holy communion

---

57 ¶ WE CAN FACILITATE OR QUENCH THE HOLY SPIRIT

Believers are called to be in harmony with the work of the Holy Spirit. Whenever people came and spoke to Jesus He would not respond to their human agenda, but would reply according to their spiritual need. The

Pharisees lived according to rigid rules and traditions, and condemned others who did not, so when a senior Pharisee named Nicodemus came to Jesus, He explained to him how, by contrast, the Holy Spirit leads God's people: 'The wind blows wherever it chooses, and you hear its sound, but do not know where it is coming from or where it is going. So it is with everyone born of the Spirit' (John 3:1-8 NIV). With varying intensity, the wind keeps blowing all the time, and likewise, those born of the Spirit can be led by the Spirit constantly. Jesus Himself lived His earthly life led by the Holy Spirit in exactly this way.

Although we are ordinary people, God does not intend that our lives be mundane. 'We have gifts that differ according to the grace given to us: if prophecy, according to your faith; if service, then serve; if teaching, then teach; if encouragement, then encourage; if giving, then give generously; if leading, then zealously; if being merciful, with cheerfulness' (Romans 12:6-8). These gifts are not assigned to individuals who become specialists, but are distributed according to the grace the Holy Spirit gives for the moment, appropriate to the needs of the people we encounter. Thus, any believer might be merciful when the opportunity arises, any might encourage, any might give generously, any might lead, any might teach. Also when believers gather together, the Holy Spirit reserves the right to choose who does what, on each occasion. The way we are to lead is by facilitating Him, allowing Him to speak through all people, so that all the glory goes to God, and not to any person.

After His resurrection Jesus told His followers: 'Do not leave Jerusalem, but wait for the gift my Father promised, which you have heard Me speak about. For John baptized with water, but in a few days you will be baptized with the Holy Spirit' (Acts 1:4-5 NIV). On the day of Pentecost the Holy Spirit came upon every person who was in the upper room. Peter quoted an Old Testament prophecy to explain to the onlookers what was happening: 'In the last days, God says, I will pour out my Spirit on all people. Your sons and daughters will prophesy, your young men will see visions, your old men will dream dreams. Even on my servants, both men and women, I will pour out my Spirit in those days, and they will prophesy' (Acts 2:17-18 NIV). Clearly God intended all believers to experience the Holy Spirit. In the Book of Acts we read that it was commonplace for the early believers to be guided by the Holy Spirit, who sent them to certain cities, warned them which places to avoid, and advised them who to associate with. Today also we are encouraged not to quench the Holy Spirit, but to confidently respond to His prompting.

---

58 ¶ We belong to one spiritual family

Through our new birth we are all part of one spiritual family, with one Father. Despite our cultural diversity and our natural incompatibilities, we belong together and we are called to love one another, especially those who are not normally given recognition within society. Paul explained this in terms of the human body: In the human body there are many members, but the eye cannot say to the hand, 'I do not need you'; nor the head to the feet, 'I do not need you.' Rather, the members of the body which seem weaker are indispensable; and the members of the body that are unpresentable, we clothe with greatest modesty. Likewise God has composed the body of Christ so that greater honour is given to the member that lacked, and all the members have the same care for one another. If one member suffers, all the members suffer; if one member is honoured, all the members rejoice (see 1 Corinthians 12:20-26). The thing we all have in common—the fact that we are loved by our heavenly Father—eclipses all our differences.

The spiritual element is real, although difficult to describe, since it is not earthly. Yet the spiritual family of God is not an abstract phenomenon, but a real and physical connection. God's spiritual family is ever increasing, as Jesus said: 'I am the good shepherd, and I know My own and My own know Me, even as the Father knows Me and I know the Father; and I lay down My life for the sheep. I have other sheep, which are not of this fold; I must bring them also, and they will hear My voice; and they will become one flock with one shepherd' (John 10:14-16 NASB). Father God has a family in mind, individuals who were chosen before the foundation of the world. Jesus alludes to this fact in His prayer: 'I have made Your name known to the people You have given Me from the world. They were Yours but You gave them to Me' (John 17:6).

When God chose Abraham, the destiny God gave him was to be a blessing to all nations: 'Abraham will surely become a great and powerful nation, and all nations on earth will be blessed through him' (Genesis 18:18). By the time of Jesus' birth, however, God's chosen people were considered to be limited to the Jews, who lived in a culture steeped in awareness of God and of old covenant law. Some viewed the gentiles with contempt, and believed themselves to be superior. As a result of Jesus' death and resurrection, and the working of the Holy Spirit, entry into the Kingdom of God was shown to be accessible to all humankind. In the following passage Paul refers to two groups, the Jews and the Gentiles, who were once alienated from each other but are now brought together within God's family: 'Christ is our peace. He made both groups into one and broke down the barrier of the dividing wall, abolishing the enmity, which is the Law of commandments and regulations, in Himself creating one new human being from the two groups, making peace and reconciling them in one body to God through the cross, by putting to death the enmity. He preached peace to you who were far away, and peace to those who were near. Through Him all have access in one Spirit to the Father' (Ephesians 2:14-18). He removed every possible division between people groups: 'By one Spirit we were all baptized into one body, whether Jews or Greeks, whether slaves or free, and we were all made to drink of one Spirit' (1 Corinthians 12:13). We are one spiritual family.

---

59 ¶ We embody the joy and peace of the Holy Spirit

Whilst certain things in life are pleasurable, pervading joy comes from the Holy Spirit: 'The Kingdom of God is not a matter of eating and drinking, but of righteousness and peace and joy in the Holy Spirit' (Romans 14:17). The beauty of this God-given joy is that it can be experienced even in difficult times: 'You became imitators of us and of the Lord, for you welcomed the message in the midst of severe suffering with the joy given by the Holy Spirit' (1 Thessalonians 1:6 NIV). Believers experience joy communing with God, as Peter commented: 'Though you have not seen Him, you love Him, and though you do not see Him now, but believe in Him, you greatly rejoice with joy inexpressible and full of glory' (1 Peter 1:8 Mounce). In addition, the early believers were so aware of their unity in the Spirit that their joy was also sparked when their fellow believers were blessed: 'Timothy has brought us good news of your faith and love, and reported that you always remember us kindly and long to see us, as we long to see you. So in all our distress and affliction we have been reassured about you, because of your faith; for now we live, if you stand firm in the Lord. How can we thank God enough for you, and for all the joy we feel for your sake before our God' (1 Thessalonians 3:6-9).

In His sermon on the mount, Jesus stated, 'Blessed are the peacemakers, for they will be called sons of God' (Matthew 5:9). In this world we are often subjected to aggression, conflict, provocation and misunderstanding, all of which can break relationships. But as God's children we are called to peace: 'If possible, so far as it depends on you, be at peace with all people' (Romans 12:18). Paul also wrote to the Corinthian church, encouraging them to cooperate with the Holy Spirit as He was working in their lives: 'Finally brothers, rejoice, strive for maturity, take courage, be like-minded, live in peace; and the God of love and peace will be with you' (2 Corinthians 13:11 Mounce). As we allow ourselves to be led by the Holy Spirit we mature into sons of God, and we become peacemakers, reflecting the nature of the God of Peace.

Whenever a believer's mind is fixed on the Holy Spirit they will experience peace with God, humanity and the earth: 'To set the mind on the flesh leads to death, but to set the mind on the Spirit brings life and peace' (Romans 8:6 Mounce).

60 ¶ WE ARE ALL PART OF ONE ROYAL PRIESTHOOD

Peter is singled out by some for special status as the foundation stone of the church, because he was the disciple whom Jesus called the rock, and Christ said He would build His church on a rock (see Matthew 16:18). Yet, it is Peter who informs us that all believers are included in one royal priesthood, making them of equal significance in the service of God. In his letter Peter uses the Greek word basileios, translated 'royal', an adjective meaning 'belonging to the king', which also occurs in Luke 7:25: 'Those who wear expensive clothing and live in luxury are found in royal palaces'. Peter uses the Greek word hierateuma, which literally means 'body of priests', twice in this letter, first in 1 Peter 2:5: 'You are being built up as a spiritual house to be a holy body of priests to offer spiritual sacrifices acceptable to God through Jesus Christ', and again in 1 Peter 2:9: 'But you are a chosen race, a royal body of priests...'. Biblical scholars denote Peter's letter as one of the general epistles in the New Testament because it is written for Christians in general, thus Peter addresses his letter to different people in different places, all of whom are chosen by God the Father, sanctified by the Holy Spirit, and purified by Christ's blood: 'Peter, an apostle of Jesus Christ, to those who reside as aliens, scattered throughout Pontus, Galatia, Cappadocia, Asia, and Bithynia, who are chosen according to the foreknowledge of God the Father, by the sanctifying work of the Spirit, to obey Jesus Christ and be sprinkled with His blood' (1 Peter 1:1-2 NASB). This illustrates that all believers are given the honour of this royal priesthood status, and therefore all carry the responsibility it brings: 'But in your hearts revere Christ as Lord. Always be prepared to give an answer to everyone who asks you to give the reason for the hope that you have. But do this with gentleness and respect' (1 Peter 3:15 NIV). It also indicates that God did not intend there to be a priest-laity divide, or a hierarchy, amongst His people: Jesus told His disciples, 'You know that the rulers in this world lord it over their people, and officials flaunt their authority over those under them. But among you it will be different. Whoever wants to be a leader among you must be your servant, and whoever wants to be first among you must be the slave of everyone else' (Mark 10:42-44 NLT). On one occasion the crowd wanted to make Jesus king, but He was unwilling to wear a worldly crown: 'Jesus, knowing that they intended to come and make him king by force, withdrew again to a mountain by Himself' (John 6:15 NIV). There was just one crown He accepted from this world—a crown of thorns, a crown of dishonour: After Jesus had been arrested, the Roman soldiers took Him into the governor's palace and gathered the whole cohort around Him. They stripped Him, put a scarlet robe on Him, twisted together a crown of thorns and put it on His head. They put a reed in His right hand, knelt before Him and mocked Him, saying 'Hail King of the Jews' (see Matthew 27:27-29).

Whilst believers are led to do different things at different times, the things they have done are not meant to become labels that define their identity, or trophies that make them important. When a believer takes on a duty to fulfil a function on a permanent basis, their obligation can become a burden. Moreover, other believers whom God might wish to fulfil those duties on other occasions are then unable to do so because that role is occupied. So, the one becomes weary and overburdened, whilst the other becomes frustrated. The call of God is for believers to live and function as a 'royal priesthood' with direct responsibility to Christ, their great high priest (see Hebrews 4:14).

61 ¶ WE ARE A NEW ORDER OF PEOPLE

The royal priesthood that Peter describes constitutes a new order of people: 'But you are a chosen people, a royal priesthood, a holy nation, God's special possession, that you may declare the praises of Him who called you out of darkness into His wonderful light. Once you were not a people, but now you are the people of God; once you had not received mercy, but now you have received mercy' (1 Peter 2:9-10 NIV).

In Christ, despite all kinds of diversity, we are now conscious of being one living 'organism'. We are connected spiritually because we recognise the presence of Christ in one another, and we interact with each other spiritually. If believers act from the domain of their soul, there will be some people they prefer, and other people they avoid. Yet, because the Spirit is incorruptible, when believers interact spiritually they are able to relate to one another as friends.

God commissioned Adam and Eve to rule over the earth and every creature (see Genesis 1:26), but not to rule over other people. The building of the tower at Babel was contrary to God's command to go forth and populate the earth, but also contrary to His heart of unity. Not only their independence from God, but also the creation of a hierarchy, with an elite destined for the higher storeys of the tower of Babel, mirrored Satan's attitude of rebellion. In response, God said: 'If as one people speaking the same language they have begun to do this, then nothing they plan to do will be impossible for them' (Genesis 11:6 NIV). At first glance this looks as if the people had unity. But because this unity was of the soul, and God knew it was destined to hurt people and oppress them rather than to work for the benefit of all and to sustain the earth, God had to stop their scheme. However, if people are in true spiritual unity, the Holy Spirit can lead them to do things far beyond their natural abilities or worldly influence. As Jesus alluded: 'With humans this is impossible, but not with God; all things are possible with God' (Mark 10:27).

Within Satan's world system, various new orders of people have been set up. These organisations use methods such as rituals, fear and coercion, to ensure their members can be trusted. In sharp contrast, when believers are led by the Holy Spirit, in communities permeated with God's love, they constitute a new order of people who are completely trustworthy, without any need of the external pressure of intimidation.

62 ¶ We are entrusted with spiritual gifts

The Holy Spirit dispenses spiritual gifts to believers for the benefit of all, in whatever way He chooses: 'There are different gifts, but the same Spirit. There are different ways to serve, but the same Lord. There are different activities, but the same God produces them all in everyone. The manifestation of the Spirit is given for the common good. To one is given through the Spirit a message of wisdom, to another a message of knowledge by the same Spirit, to another faith by the same Spirit, to another gifts of healing by that one Spirit, to another effecting miracles, to another prophecy, to another discerning spirits, to another speaking in different tongues, and to another the interpretation of tongues. All these are the work of one and the same Spirit, and He distributes them to each one, just as He determines' (1 Corinthians 12:4-11). These gifts were not intended merely to be operational in religious gatherings. Believers were to be ready to use the gifts in any context, at the prompting of the Holy Spirit, in the same way Jesus did. The tasks believers are given by the Holy

Spirit, as He guides them, all work together to help every believer grow and mature into their full potential and personal responsibility before God, or to reveal God to people who do not yet know Him: 'Christ gave the apostles, the prophets, the evangelists, the pastors and teachers, to equip the saints for the work of service, to build up of the body of Christ, until we all attain to the unity of the faith and of the knowledge of the Son of God, to full maturity, to the greatest measure of the abundance of Christ. Then we will no longer be children, tossed to and fro and blown about by every wind of doctrine, by the trickery of men, by craftiness in deceitful scheming' (Ephesians 4:7-14). Paul explains here that as believers grow in maturity they will not feel the need to run after the latest spiritual fad, nor will they be fooled by man-made doctrines.

When believers experience success in operating a spiritual gift, they may be tempted to imagine they are rising above their brothers and sisters in their usefulness to God. But Jesus explains that whenever anyone bears spiritual fruit the Father wishes to prune them so they will bear fruit in another season: 'I am the true vine, and My Father is the vinedresser. Every branch in Me that does not bear fruit, He takes away; and every branch that bears fruit, He prunes it so that it may bear more fruit' (John 15:1-3 NASB). Unpruned vines which are allowed to grow long tendrils and produce beautiful leaves are very attractive to the human eye, but they only produce a few tiny, inedible grapes that do not ripen. In working vineyards, vines are cut back severely until they look like ugly gnarled sticks, very unattractive, but these produce abundant fruit: 'My Father is glorified by this, that you bear much fruit, and become My disciples' (John 15:8). God knows that whenever our spiritual activity brings human accolade there is real danger that we become proud and are deceived into thinking we are spiritually superior to others. Thus Christ recommends we become, and remain, like little children. Spiritual gifts and callings are given to bring glory to Father God, never to make believers special. Thus, whilst we are encouraged to eagerly desire spiritual gifts we need to remember it is by the fruit of the Spirit, which is the character of Christ, that we are known to God.

---

63 ¶ We continue His work

Believers continue the work of Christ on earth, as they are led by the Spirit. This could be compared to them being used as God's pens with which He writes His imprint on the earth. In museums you sometimes see the old style wooden school desk used by earlier generations, dating from the 1950s back to the 1800s. These desks had a sloping flip-up lid with a space for storing books beneath, and on the top, a sliding brass plate concealing a small ceramic ink-well. Before each lesson the teacher would go round the classroom filling up all the ink-wells. The pens the children used were very simple, comprising a wooden handle with a curved metal nib—no cartridge or reservoir as in a fountain pen, as these were expensive items at the time. This old fashioned system of writing was potentially very messy because the pens would often need to be dipped into the ink to be recharged, and children had to be very careful.

God has a lot of writing to do. The world we live in is the paper He wants to use. He wants us to allow Him to use us as His pens. This means we rest in His hand, not wriggling about and pulling in other directions as He takes us over the paper. The Holy Spirit is the ink. The only writing that will remain indelible is the kind that uses this ink. All our own works or activities, or even books we write, are going to fade away. Because if we are not dipped in the Holy Spirit ink, though we may have made all the right shapes as we passed over the paper, we will have nothing to show for it when we have finished. How disappointing that would be: 'For whoever has, to him more shall be given, and he will have an abundance; but whoever does not have, even what he has shall be taken away from him' (Matthew 13:12 NASB). With this old-fashioned kind of pen, we find we can only write a few words before we run out of ink, then we have to dip again into the Holy Spirit, write a few more words, then dip again, write, dip again—it is a rhythm, and one we are unfamiliar with in the modern world. We are more comfortable with instant ballpoint pen writing, self-sufficiency, being in control. But God has arranged it so that our work for Him and our intimacy with Him are intertwined.

We also see this principle at work in the way Jesus lived; He was regularly led to withdraw from people and go away alone to spend time in prayer with His Father, and He always found Himself to be in the right place at the right time—He simply walked into situations already set up for Him, and the glory of God was revealed each time. This can also apply to believers who respond to the gentle prompting of the Holy Spirit, wherever they happen to be: 'We are God's workmanship, created in Christ Jesus for good works which God prepared beforehand so that we would walk in them' (Ephesians 2:10).

Our human nature tends to make us think that high-profile events, and large scale Christian programmes are of the greatest value in advancing the Kingdom of God. Such initiatives are widely admired, and many believers wish to be associated with them, contributing their own efforts, time and money to them. But Jesus has a less grandiose expectation of us: A word of kindness, or a small act of generosity, when initiated by the Holy Spirit, might be of even greater value than preaching to thousands of people. Jesus sees our efforts differently, highly valuing things we may regard as insignificant: 'Whoever can be trusted with very little can also be trusted with much, and whoever is dishonest with very little will also be dishonest with much' (Luke 16:10). Jesus even explained that on judgment day, to some He will say: 'I was hungry and you gave me something to eat; I was thirsty and you gave me a drink; I was a stranger and you invited me in; naked and you clothed me; I was sick and you visited me; I was in prison and you came to me', explaining 'Whenever you did it to these brothers of mine, even to the least of them, you did it to me' (Matthew 25:35-40). So, in Jesus' estimation the little things are really the big things, and people who are considered to be least important are the ones Jesus identifies Himself with. Believers are able to continue the work of Christ by simply keeping in close communion with Him, and not discounting themselves.

64 ¶ We participate in holy communion

On the night that Jesus was betrayed He ate a meal with His disciples; He took the bread and after giving thanks, broke it, gave it to them, and said, 'This is My body which is for you. Do this in remembrance of Me'. After the meal, in the same way He also took the cup, saying, 'This cup is the new covenant in My blood. Do this, as often as you drink it, in remembrance of Me' (see 1 Corinthians 11:24-25). Through holy communion, the Spirit of God reminds us of the high price Jesus paid for us, and our indebtedness. We should remember to be thankful, but human beings are forgetful, and holy communion helps to refocus us: 'As often as you do this, do it in remembrance of me'. The Greek word used here for 'remembrance' is 'anamnesis' which is closely related to our word amnesia. Anamnesis is like an antidote to amnesia. Because we get distracted by life's pressures and activities, we are prone to forget the impact that Christ's death and resurrection has had on our lives. Yet this is where our eternal life has its origin. Jesus' death on the cross was an event in eternity, not only in time. Consequently, in that moment when a person first encounters Christ, the cross becomes a present reality, as well as a historical fact.

Christ's body gives us life: "'I am the bread of life. Your fathers ate the manna in the wilderness, and they died. This is the bread which comes down out of heaven, so that one may eat of it and not die. I am the living bread that came down out of heaven; if anyone eats of this bread, he will live forever; and the bread also which I will give for the life of the world is My flesh." Then the Jews began to argue with one another, saying, "How can this man give us His flesh to eat?" So Jesus said to them, "Truly, truly, I say to you, unless you eat the flesh of the Son of Man and drink His blood, you have no life in yourselves. He who eats My flesh and drinks My blood has eternal life, and I will raise him up on the last day. For My flesh is true food, and My blood is true drink. He who eats My flesh and drinks My blood abides in Me, and I in him. As the living Father sent Me, and I live because of the Father, so he who eats Me, he also will live because of Me. This is the bread which came down out of heaven; not as the fathers ate and died; he who eats this bread will live forever."' (John 6:48-48 NASB). There is a parallel here between the first Adam, who brought death to the human race as a result of eating the fruit of the tree of the knowledge of good-and-evil, and Jesus, the 'last Adam,' who gives life to believers as a result of eating His body.

The act of holy communion reminds believers of what Christ has achieved through the cross, and connects them to heaven. Communion, therefore, is not merely a symbol, but Christ gives us something tangible that we actually take into our mortal bodies. By faith, we then receive His body as true spiritual food, and His blood as true spiritual drink. The substance of the bread and wine is not the point: Jesus said of the elements of bread and wine, 'This is my body, this is my blood' whilst He was still living in His human body. This is a mystery, but we experience the same spiritual benefit from eating His body and drinking His blood as did the disciples with whom Jesus shared His last Passover supper. During that meal Jesus was pointing forward to His sacrificial death when He said, 'This is my body broken for you, this is my blood poured out for you'. We need spiritual sustenance on a regular basis, and it is unwise to underestimate its importance. Through holy communion the Holy Spirit encourages believers to focus on the sacrifice Christ made, and He reawakens their gratitude to Christ, who became incarnate as the Passover lamb who gave His life for us.

LOVE: CHANGING US TO BE LIKE CHRIST

A WORK OF FATHER GOD

9

THE NATURE OF FATHER GOD

65. He is the only Father and He is in heaven
66. He loves us unconditionally
67. He is not angry with humanity
68. He has only good intentions toward us
69. He so loved the world that He gave His
    only Son
70. He is the Father of the fatherless
71. He is exactly like Jesus
72. He knows everything about us

65 ¶ HE IS THE ONLY FATHER AND HE IS IN HEAVEN

Father God resides in heaven, and Jesus encourages
us to relate to Him: 'When you pray, go into your room,
close the door and pray to your Father, who is unseen.
Then your Father, who sees what is done in secret, will

reward you. And when you pray, do not keep on babbling like pagans, for they think they will be heard because of their many words. Do not be like them, for your Father knows what you need before you ask Him. This, then, is how you should pray: 'Our Father in heaven…' (see Matthew 9:6-9).

The Father relates to us as His children, and this is different from His relationship with the angels. The angels are an older order of God's creatures; they are mighty, glorious, knowledgeable and immortal—but some of them, trusting in their own beauty and power, rebelled against God, led by Satan. After this rebellion, God created humankind out of the dust, breathing His own breath into us to impart life. Compared with angels, we are a very different order of creature; we are dependent, vulnerable, naive and mortal. We were made to need God's love, His affirmation, His wisdom—we need Him. There is a genealogy of Jesus in Luke 3 which goes back through the generations all the way to Adam, finally stating '…Seth was the son of Adam, and Adam was the son of God' (Luke 3:38). Adam and Eve were parented by Father God, thus the original Father was actually Father God. But through the fall, this intimate bond was broken. In fact, no son of Adam can ever be a perfect parent because we were not designed to do the job. So if your parents were not perfect, it is because their parents were not perfect parents to them, and their parents were not perfect parents to them… and so on, through the generations all the way back to Adam. And it may well be true to say that every generation blames the one before. Thus it is important to understand how this works, and to bypass our parents and get back to the original, perfect parent—which is Father God. This is how it was actually intended to work. Receiving revelation that God is our own Father is imperative for discovering our true identity, as Paul wrote: 'For this reason I bow my knees before the Father, from whom every family in heaven and on earth derives its name' (Ephesians 3:14-15 NASB).

---

66 ¶ HE LOVES US UNCONDITIONALLY

The Father's love for us is not dependent upon our performance, whether in deed or thought, or what we fail to do, whether in the past, present or future. His love is therefore completely unconditional. In order to please Him, however, we need to have faith in Christ. After His miracle to feed five thousand people, Jesus told the crowd to work for food that endures to everlasting life. These people were familiar with the Law of Moses, which required offerings and rituals as the means of pleasing God. Therefore they asked Jesus what works they needed to perform. Jesus answered, 'This is the work God wants from you, that you believe in Him whom He sent' (see John 6:28-29). Jesus explained to His disciples how their faith in Him is connected to the Father's love, and He reassured them that after He had ascended to heaven, the Father's love would not diminish: 'In that day you will ask in My name, and I do not say to you that I will request of the Father on your behalf; for the Father Himself loves you, because you have loved Me and have believed that I came forth from the Father' (John 16:26-27 NASB). Each of us was created, first and foremost, to be the object of Father God's love. There are times, of course, when we do not particularly feel that we are being loved, such as when we are struggling with difficult circumstances. Yet when we are led by the Spirit, whatever is needed is provided by the Father, and we have a sense of being loved: 'You did not choose Me but I chose you, and appointed you that you would go and bear fruit, and that your fruit would remain, so that whatever you ask of the Father in My name He may give to you' (John 15:16 NASB). His love is unconditional, and it is unstoppable.

67 ¶ HE IS NOT ANGRY WITH HUMANITY

God's anger is not aimed at humanity, but at the forces of darkness. And He desires that believers also refrain from directing their anger toward human beings, as they recognise that evil human behaviour is spiritually instigated: 'Our struggle is not against flesh and blood, but against the rulers, against the powers, against the world forces of this darkness, against the spiritual forces of evil in the heavenly places' (Ephesians 6:12).

God was not even angry with Adam for the fall of humankind itself. He had warned Adam not to eat from the tree of the knowledge of good-and-evil, 'because in the day that you eat from it you will surely die' (Genesis 2:17). But Adam and Eve chose to follow the suggestion of the serpent rather than heed God's warning, and they ate the fruit: Immediately their eyes were opened and they knew they were naked, so they sewed fig leaves together, and made themselves loin coverings. They heard the sound of the Lord God walking in the garden, and hid themselves amongst the trees. God was not angry and did not hide Himself from them. They explained to Him what had happened, and God helped them in their immediate predicament—He made garments of skin for Adam and his wife, and clothed them. God spoke words over the serpent, which declared His solution to the damage the serpent inflicted on the human race: 'I will put enmity between you and the woman, and between your seed and her Seed; He shall bruise you on the head, and you shall bruise Him on the heel' (Genesis 3:15). These words prophesied the incarnation of Jesus, who was the 'Seed' born of a woman, who would come to earth to redeem humanity. After this, God sent Adam and Eve out from the garden of Eden in order to prevent them eating the fruit of the tree of life. This was not a punishment but a safeguard, for had they eaten from the tree of life, they would have been doomed to lived for eternity in their fallen state: 'And the Lord God said, "The man has now become like one of Us, knowing good and evil. He must not be allowed to reach out his hand and take also from the tree of life and eat, and live forever." So the Lord God banished him from the Garden of Eden to work the ground from which he had been taken' (Genesis 3:22-23 NIV). When God prevented Adam and Eve from eating this fruit it was also His mercy, to ensure that they remained mortal—then there would be hope of redemption for humankind. The heart of the Father is set on the lost; He is not angry with them, but continuously longs for their return.

---

68 ¶ HE HAS ONLY GOOD INTENTIONS TOWARD US

In the light of Father God's good intentions towards us, non-believers who hear the story of the fall might well question why God would set up Adam and Eve for failure. It is commonly taught that the first sin ever committed was disobedience to God. The story goes along these lines: Adam and Eve disregarded God's advice to not eat the fruit of the tree of the knowledge of good-and-evil, and as a result of their disobedience, Adam and Eve became afraid of God and hid from Him, then shortly afterwards they were removed from Eden to prevent them eating from the Tree of Life. This has been misinterpreted to imply that God is punishing humanity for this act of disobedience, by separating Himself from us.

However, there is evidence that God has such high regard for the free will He gives us that He does not cut off our relationship with Himself, even if we do choose to disobey His instructions. This fact is illustrated in the story of Jonah in the Old Testament. Jonah was in relationship with God, but when God told him to travel to Nineveh and preach repentance to the people of the city, he refused to go. Jonah knew God to be merciful, and he so disliked the Ninevites that he did not want to give them the chance to repent. He got on a boat sailing in the opposite direction. God's response was not to reject Jonah, but rather He put in motion a sequence of miraculous events designed to persuade Jonah to see things from God's point of view. At the end of the story we see Jonah and God still in close relationship, with God patiently teaching Jonah about compassion.

By contrast, in 1 Kings 13 there is a story about a 'man of God from Judah' who is not specifically named. God told this man to prophesy in the presence of King Jeroboam, then return home by a different way, without eating or drinking. This man did exactly as God instructed, until an old prophet deceived him, telling him an angel had spoken, saying the young man should eat and drink with the old prophet. The 'man of God from Judah' listened to the old prophet instead of continuing to believe God. He switched his obedience from God to a human being, and as a consequence he died. The point of these two stories is not to suggest that God favours one servant over the other. He chose both men despite their weaknesses, and for God, the development of the messengers' character is as important as their mission. Both these men were disobedient, yet God did not stop loving them. However, whenever a believer puts their trust in another person whom they regard as spiritually superior, rather than staying faithful to what they have heard from God, they jeopardise their own spiritual progress.

God gave Adam and Eve the gift of free will. There were no laws or rules in the Garden of Eden. They had freedom to choose, even if they chose to eat from the Tree of the knowledge of good-and-evil. In the Garden they were not living in obedience to anyone, they were living in loving relationship. The sin they committed was that they complied with the suggestion of another, which was actually obedience to the serpent, who is Satan. As descendants of Adam, the human race, being deceived, has unwittingly obeyed Satan ever since. The consequences of sin are the consequences of obeying Satan, not the consequences of disobeying God. The Mosaic Law was given many centuries later in order to redirect the obedience of God's chosen people away from Satan, and toward God. Thus God's intentions toward humanity were always good.

God intentionally desires the best in believers' lives: "'For I know the plans I have for you," declares the Lord, "plans to prosper you and not to harm you, plans to give you hope and a future"' (Jeremiah 29:11). His care also extends to our difficult times: 'All praise to God, the Father of our Lord Jesus Christ. He is our merciful Father and the God of all encouragement, who encourages us in all our afflictions so that we can encourage others when they are in any affliction, with the same encouragement God has given us' (see 2 Corinthians 1:3-4). In fact, He uses these times for our ultimate good: 'God causes all things to work together for good to those who love God, to those who are called according to His purpose. If God is for us, who is against us? He who did not spare His own Son, but delivered Him over for us all, how will He not also with Him freely give us all things?' (Romans 8:28, 31-32 NASB). Father God loves all His children and desires their spiritual maturity.

---

69 ¶ HE SO LOVED THE WORLD THAT HE GAVE HIS ONLY SON

'For God loved the world so much that He gave His only Son so that anyone who believes in Him shall not perish but have eternal life' (John 3:16). It could be argued that the crucifixion demonstrates there is nothing human beings can do to stop the Father loving us, since the execution of His blameless Son is the most devastating thing that humankind could perpetrate against the Father, yet He loves us still.

However, we contend that there is a false teaching that the Father needed to satisfy His 'wrath' by hurting His Son. This teaching empowers the strategy of Satan, who wants people to mistrust the Father's motives—the same trick that Satan used with Adam and Eve in the garden of Eden. The following scripture describes the impact of the atoning sacrifice God has given us: 'By this the love of God was manifested in us, that God has sent His only begotten Son into the world so that we might live through Him. In this is love, not that we loved God, but that He loved us and sent His Son to be the propitiation for our sins' (1 John 4:9-10 NASB). The translator of this passage renders the Greek word 'hilasmos' as propitiation for our sins, which describes the atoning sacrifice of Christ. As the following verses explain: 'And although you were dead in your trespasses and the uncircumcision of your flesh, God made you alive with Christ. He forgave us all our transgressions, having cancelled the certificate of debt with its legal demands against us, which was hostile to us. He has taken it away by nailing it to the cross. He stripped the principalities and powers of their authority, and disgraced them in public by triumphing over them in Christ' (Colossians 2:13-15 Mounce). Thus we understand that Satan keeps his own record of our sins, which he holds against us. Christ annulled Satan's hostile record, nailing it to the cross. Part of the deception of the fall is man's mistaken idea that God is hostile toward them on account of their transgressions. However, it is not God who accuses us, but Satan. In another sense, the crucifixion was an atoning sacrifice that removed man's mistrust of God, without presupposing God's wrath needed to be satisfied.

Paul explains to believers: 'When you were slaves to sin, you were free from the control of righteousness. What benefit did you reap at that time from the things you are now ashamed of? Those things result in death! But now that you have been set free from sin and have become slaves of God, the benefit you reap leads to holiness, and the result is eternal life. For the wages of sin is death, but the gift of God is eternal life in Christ Jesus our Lord' (Romans 6:20-23 NIV). Sin itself is deceitful (see Hebrews 3:13). We get lied to when we are tempted, then we believe the lie and act on it, and if this is not checked it will eventually lead to death. This works in a similar way to somebody being told there is no greater experience than a heroin 'trip', but they are not told that the consequences of using heroin will eventually be destructive. If this principle is applied to all sin in the world, we can then see that unredeemed people, as a result of deception, are on the path the destruction, because Satan deceives in order to steal, kill and destroy. Knowing humanity's propensity for being deceived into sinning, God intervened with the sacrifice of His Son, 'who takes away the sin of the world' (see John 1:29). One thing is clear—it is not the purpose of the cross to satisfy 'God's wrath', because if Jesus' death had appeased God's anger with sin, the Father would no longer be troubled by the sin that continues in the world. But He is. The work of the cross was not directed at the Father, and was not intended to change something about Him. On the contrary, the Father has provided a rescue plan for those who believe. And we can also trust that He will deal with sin justly: 'Never take your own revenge, beloved, but leave room for the wrath of God, for it is written, "Vengeance is mine, I will repay, says the Lord."' (Romans 12:19 NASB).

The purpose of the Father giving His Son was to reconnect humankind with Himself, and to reverse the effects of the fall. A non-believer might argue that because God created the world, which was then subjected to the fall, He could and should have simply reversed the process, rather than letting us all go through the misery, including sacrificing His Son. However, had God merely 'reset' the world and undone the fall, Satan would have plotted humankind's downfall again. So, since Satan continues to exist on earth, there was in fact no other way to rescue humanity from their propensity to capitulate to the devil, other than to provide an alternative 'Adam' who was able to impart life: 'In Adam all die, but in Christ all are made alive' (see 1 Corinthians 15:22 & 45). This was fully accomplished through the incarnation of Jesus, who refused to acquiesce to Satan's enticements, intimidation, or torture, even to the ultimate extreme of death.

70 ¶ HE IS THE FATHER OF THE FATHERLESS

'God is a Father to the fatherless' (see Psalm 68:5), and this has always been true of Him. When God calls Himself the Father of the fatherless He does not mean He merely wants to adopt those whose fathers have died, but that He has a special place in His heart for those whose fathers and mothers did not love them properly, did not value them enough, did not have time for them, or were not interested in them. Whenever the job of fathering or mothering was not conducted properly, then God's Father-heart is especially moved with compassion. Yet without Father God, everyone is in a sense 'fatherless' even if they had the best parents. In the world, many people without God sense their own fatherlessness, which causes them to experience insecurity, loneliness, hopelessness and lack of identity. This often drives people to create their own significance and identity, in all kinds of unhelpful ways.

It is important to understand how God intended that families should function. Natural parents do not own their children, but in reality God owns all the babies who are born. The natural parents have a God-given stewardship to bring up their children on God's behalf. And God's ideal is that children should be affirmed and given love by the parents, so that all the potential which God put inside them before they were born will develop into its fullness. It may be obvious, but it is true to say that men are not born fathers—they become fathers because a woman is having their baby. They might be happy about it, or they might be upset about it. For some people, in their parents' eyes they were 'a mistake', but Father God has always wanted us, and waited for us. To the Ephesians Paul writes: 'God our Father…has blessed us with every spiritual blessing in the heavenly places in Christ, just as He chose us in Him before the foundation of the world' (Ephesians 1:3-4 NASB). Unlike men, our heavenly Father was always a father—His identity is Father; His name is Father; His job is to father His children—we are His workmanship (see Ephesians 2:10) so when He goes to work, His job is to change us, so we progressively become like Jesus. Our Heavenly Father simply has two desires: First, for His children to know Him as their Father, and second, that each one will grow to become like Jesus: 'Those whom God foreknew, He also predestined to be conformed to the image of His Son, that He might be the firstborn among many brothers and sisters' (Romans 8:29).

---

71 ¶ He is exactly like Jesus

Jesus told His disciples, 'If you had known Me, you would have known My Father also; from now on you know Him, and have seen Him.' Philip said to Him, 'Lord, show us the Father, and it is enough for us.' Jesus said to him, 'Have I been so long with you, and yet you have not come to know Me, Philip? He who has seen Me has seen the Father; how can you say, Show us the Father? Do you not believe that I am in the Father, and the Father is in Me? The words that I say to you I do not speak on My own initiative, but the Father abiding in Me does His works. Believe Me that I am in the Father and the Father is in Me' (John 14:7-11 NASB). It is interesting that even in different cultures and faiths, Jesus is acknowledged as an exemplary humble, kind, wise and virtuous person. These qualities fully exhibit the nature of Father God, as Jesus explained: 'I and the Father are one' (John 10:30).

The Father's nature has often been misunderstood as harsh and faultfinding, but this is a fallacy, as even the following Old Testament passage illustrates: 'Does the Lord take delight in thousands of rams, in ten thousand rivers of oil? Shall I present my firstborn for my rebellious acts, the fruit of my body for the sin of my soul? He has told you, O man, what is good; and what does the Lord require of you but to do justice, to love kindness, and to walk humbly with your God?' (Micah 6:7-8 NASB). Yet churches often teach that Father God abandoned Jesus when He was at His lowest point, based on Jesus crying out on the cross, 'Eli, Eli Lama Sabacthani' which is Aramaic for 'My God, my God, why have you forsaken me?' As an attempt to explain this utterance it is sometimes incorrectly taught that Jesus became sin, and Father God cannot look on sin, therefore He had to forsake Him. Yet God can and does observe sin all the time, as well as its impact on humanity and the earth, so this view can be discounted. The Greek word for sin, and sin offering, are interchangeable, which has given scope for people to interpret the scripture as 'Jesus becoming sin'. Yet this view contradicts the notion of Christ as an innocent sacrifice. The scriptures clearly teach that Christ came as the pure unblemished Lamb of God: 'For Christ, our Passover lamb, has been sacrificed' (1 Corinthians 5:7), in other words, Jesus was a 'sin offering', which has a very different inference from becoming 'sin'.

The reason for Christ's exclamation is better understood without ever suggesting the Trinity could be divided. Jesus was crying out the first line of Psalm 22, 'Eli, Eli, lama sabachthani?'. But He was not exhibiting self pity; nor was He accusing the Father of abandoning Him; nor was He affirming the taunts of the scoffers who were suggesting He was forsaken by God. Matthew's gospel records this abuse: The chief priests, along with the scribes and elders, mocked Him, saying, "He saved others but He is not able to save Himself. He is supposed to be the King of Israel, so let Him come down from the cross and we will believe in Him. He said He trusts in God, so let God rescue Him if He delights in Him, because He said, 'I am the Son of God.'" (Matthew 27:41-43). But the Psalm specifically poses the question, 'Why?' We know the reason Christ needed to be made fully human: He became an alternative Adam to be a champion on behalf of all humanity, and in that capacity

He never capitulated to the devil. The incarnation was the Trinity's strategy to provide human beings with a means of release from their enslavement to Satan's deception. However, insufficient consideration has been given to why Christ felt a sense of separation.

The first Adam was created as a being that was not originally meant to die, and his spirit, soul and body were continually communing with God in unison. Yet he was warned that if he ate from the tree of the knowledge of good-and-evil he would die. When Adam was tempted by the devil he decided to trust Satan's words, and ate from this tree. It was his soul that made this decision, and as a result, his soul gained ascendancy over his spirit. Immediately his soul lost its consciousness of God, his body was exposed to the effects of death, and his spirit was constrained by his now dominant soul.

Jesus was incarnated as 'the last Adam', a new beginning, parallel to the state of the first Adam before the fall. Jesus' soul, spirit and body were continuously communing with God the Father, and the Holy Spirit. Since Jesus never ate the fruit of the tree of the knowledge of good-and-evil, nor committed any sin, He could not naturally die. The Romans nailed Jesus' body to the cross; throughout His crucifixion Jesus' spirit was communing with the Father and the Holy Spirit, until He gave His spirit into His Father's hands at the very end. Jesus' soul, however, was drawing upon God the Father as the source of life; His soul therefore had to be disconnected from this source of life in order to release Him to undergo an authentic human death. At that moment of disconnection, Jesus, in His soul, became painfully conscious of the separation.

Father God and Jesus have never worked apart from one another, and this is true of every word, act of kindness and decision. There never was, and never could be, any division in the Trinity.

---

72 ¶ He knows everything about us

The Father is the only one who knows us completely, and loves us as we truly are—we do not have to do anything, or behave in a particular way, to persuade Him to love us. He is not impressed with our religious performance, or whether we attend church meetings, but He sees right through our masks, to the condition of our heart. He knows everything we have suffered, what are our secret fears, as well as the deceptions that drive us into false behaviours when we interact with other people. In a sense, it is comforting to realise that God already knows the worst about us, and even now He is fully aware of all the motives of our heart, although we are not yet conscious of these ourselves.

No human being, however intimate they may be, can ever understand us as He does. He knows how many hairs we have on our head (see Matthew 10:29-31), and He has written our name on His hand: 'Can a woman forget her nursing child and have no compassion on the son of her womb? Even these may forget, but I will not forget you. Behold, I have inscribed you on the palms of My hands' (Isaiah 49:15-16 NASB). There is a special part of God's heart that belongs only to me. And God has a special part of His heart that belongs only to you—not to anyone else. This is true for each one of His children. Some people did not get much personal attention from their parents because they had to share them with brothers and sisters. But our Heavenly Father gives you all His attention. He never compares His children with each other, like earthly parents do, 'Why can't you be more like your sister?' No, He treats each one of us as if we were His only child.

The Father longs for you to connect with His heart—remember that nobody else can touch that part of His heart which belongs to you, and if you do not come to Him, then He will be lonely for you. He longs for you to come to Him like a small child and just rest and let Him love you, not to try and please Him. This is why He says: 'Be still, and know that I am God' (Psalm 46:10). Believers are safe in the knowledge that He knows and understands them completely.

THE DESIRE OF FATHER GOD

73. He wants us to love Him with all our being
74. He wants us to see each other the way Christ sees us
75. He does not want anyone to perish
76. He wants us conformed to the character of His Son
77. He wants us to live in Spirit and truth
78. He wants us to be free of the world's delusions
79. He wants to instigate our destiny
80. He will not override the human will

---

73 ¶ HE WANTS US TO LOVE HIM WITH ALL OUR BEING
God the Father, first and foremost, desires our love, as expressed in His most important commandment:

'Love the Lord your God with all your heart and with all your soul and with all your mind and with all your strength' (Mark 12:30 NIV). The more we think about this commandment, the more we realise how amazing it is: If a boy and girl are going out together, and the boy realises he is in love with the girl, he will have to find the courage to tell her. But he will feel very vulnerable because she might not feel the same way about him. When you tell someone 'I love you' you risk being rejected, being laughed at, even losing the person. It is truly a risky thing to do. However, one thing you are most unlikely to do is to say to a person 'I want you to love me': If you said that it would make you doubly vulnerable, and people would say to you, 'Haven't you got any pride?'. But this is exactly what Father God says to us; He says 'I want you to love me'. The God who created the universe opens up His heart to us and makes Himself totally vulnerable to His creatures. God gives us His heart without guarding Himself from the pain of rejection because He has a passion for us that we hardly begin to understand. We see this passion when He gives His precious Son to die on the cross— His only Son. Can you imagine how that feels? Even if you have several children can you imagine giving up one to death? The agony suffered by a parent seeing his only child being killed before his very eyes is worse than the parent himself dying. However, Father God was willing to go through the most awful emotional pain possible. This can only begin make sense to us when we understand the depth of God's determination to win back our love.

Paul describes the passion the early believers had for God: 'If we seem crazy, we are crazy for God; if we are sensible it is for you, because we are constrained by the love of Christ. We have come to the conclusion that, since One has died for all, all have therefore died. And He died for us all so that we who are living might no longer live for ourselves, but for the One who died and was raised for us' (see 2 Corinthians 5:13-15). Jesus pointed out that those who are forgiven much, love much (see Luke 7:47), and perhaps this is the reason that 'there is more joy in heaven over one sinner who repents than over ninety-nine righteous persons who do not need to repent' (Luke 15:7). God longs for us to reciprocate His love.

---

74 ¶ He wants us to see each other the way Christ sees us

Father God wants believers to see one another through the eyes of Christ. Mother Teresa of Calcutta said: 'Whenever I meet someone in need, it is really Jesus in His most distressing disguise' (Mother Teresa, *Where There is Love, There is God* New York: Doubleday, 2010). With all her heart she determined to live out the gospel. Jesus said: 'Truly I tell you, whatever you did for one of the least of these brothers and sisters of Mine, you did for Me' (Matthew 25:40). Christ identifies Himself with people the world considers as 'the least', and He desires that we value all people as He does, without distinctions: If one person comes to your meeting wearing expensive clothes, and someone else turns up in dirty old clothes, and you make a fuss over the person who looks rich, but ignore the poor person, that is discrimination, and you are acting like uncaring judges. God chose the poor of this world to be rich in faith, and to inherit the kingdom He promised to those who love Him (see James 2:1-5). Additionally, God does not want believers to regard themselves as inferior or superior: Let the brother of lowly circumstances rejoice in his high position; and let the wealthy brother rejoice in his low position, because both will disappear like flowers in the grass (see James 1:9-10).

Paul determined to see beyond believers' earthly status and condition, instead looking for Christ within them (see 2 Corinthians 5:16). Acknowledging that each person is on their own spiritual journey with God, he advised believers to be tolerant of others' spiritual blind spots: If you notice that a believer has a weakness in his faith, treat him with kindness, and do not show him up. One person may have received revelation that God has permitted him to eat anything, but another person who has not received that revelation will still restrict himself to food allowed by the Law of Moses. The one with freedom should not regard with contempt the one who restrains himself; nor should the one who restrains himself judge the one who eats freely. God accepts both of them, and believers are always in the wrong whenever they presume to judge the servants of God (see Romans 14:1-4). When believers behave with spiritual immaturity this is often the result of the wounds, fears or deceptions which have been inflicted upon them, which God will heal in due course. So judging, or even criticising other Christians is outside our remit. Whilst the apostle Paul diligently advised each church against ungodliness, he did not disclose to one church what any other church was doing wrong.

The issue of judgment is often misunderstood by believers. A judge's duty is not only to help determine whether a law has been transgressed, but also to pass an appropriate sentence. However, when believers are instructed not to judge, this does not mean they must accept everything without critical judgment, otherwise Jesus' advice that we should not cast our pearls before 'swine' would be meaningless. It is the sentencing aspect of judgment which all believers are called to avoid, whether this means giving somebody the 'cold shoulder', burning them at the stake, or as in the passage above, regarding them with contempt.

God wants believers to understand that we all need one another, thus we are encouraged never to imagine ourselves as more important than the others: Do not get big ideas about your own importance, but regard yourself with a humble mind, since God has allotted a portion of faith to everyone. Just as our human body has many members, each with its unique function, likewise all of us are one body in Christ, and individually members one of another (see Romans 12:3-5).

The fleshly divisions amongst us are mostly a result of the random circumstances of our birth, but have no significance in respect of our 'new man', born of the Spirit of God: We are all sons of God through faith in Christ, and we are no longer Jew or Greek, slave or free, male or female (see Galatians 3:26-28). In actual fact, believers were (and still are) Jews and Greeks, slaves and free, and also male and female. Naturally, our experiences of life can cause us to view different types of people in prejudiced ways, but Father God wants us to relate to one another as the new creation we actually are—sons of God. Historically, women have often been regarded as less important than men. After Adam and Eve sinned in the Garden of Eden, God spoke a curse over the serpent: 'And I will put enmity between you (Satan) and the woman, and between your seed and her Seed' (Genesis 3:15). But it was never God's intention that there would be enmity between men and women. However, Satan has gone to great lengths to stir up misogyny within his world system in order to express his own hatred toward women, and to cause fundamental division within humankind. Yet believers are called to transcend the lie of misogyny, since Christ has overcome the power of Satan's works: A husband must honour his wife, treating her with understanding, so that his prayers will not be hindered. She may be physically weaker, but she is a co-heir of God's gift of life (see 1 Peter 3:7).

As God's children we are also called to equally value non-believers because we do not know whose names have been written in 'the Lamb's book of life from the foundation of the world' (see Revelation 17:8 and Philippians 4:3). Anyone is a potential child of God, because Jesus laid down His life for all. Therefore we are encouraged not to judge those who do not believe, but to view them through the eyes of God.

75 ¶ HE DOES NOT WANT ANYONE TO PERISH

Salvation is intended for all. Right at the start of the bible we read about the origin of human sin. God made humankind in His own image and prepared a wonderful garden for him to live in—everything was perfect. So, who thought up the terrible idea of eating the fruit that causes death? It was not Adam's idea and it was not Eve's idea—they were both fine with things as they were. It was Satan's scheme. Now Satan is a fallen angel; but he was created beautiful, powerful, clever—then he chose to serve his own Ego instead of serving God (see Ezekiel 28:14-17). Satan is outraged that God has had the audacity to create a new type of being in His own image. And he is even more outraged that God has chosen to honour and cherish human beings above the angelic beings. It is as if Satan says to himself, 'These humans are contemptible weaklings, they're fools, virtually scraps of meat. If I'm going down, I'll take them down with me'. And Satan is going down, because despite seeing God's glory and loving kindness, he became dazzled by his own splendour and imagined he could take God's place (see Isaiah 14:13-15). Jesus refers to 'The eternal fire which has been prepared for the devil and his angels' (Matthew 25:41), but from the beginning this was not intended for human beings. Satan knows exactly what sin does: sin separates the guilty one from God; and Satan knows exactly what unforgiveness does: unforgiveness separates the victim of sin from God. Therefore Satan incites people to sin and to hold unforgiveness.

In Genesis 2 God had already explained that if Adam were to eat the fruit of the tree of good-and-evil he would certainly die. This is like telling a child: 'Do not drink the bleach under the sink or it will kill you'. It is a warning, not a threat. When God spoke, things were created. God spoke into place a system of morality, and all the laws of the universe, which hold all things together in perfect balance. God cannot simply reverse what He has declared, otherwise the universe might disintegrate. In respect of sin, He has declared that 'the wages of sin is death' (Romans 6:23). The word 'wages' is interesting. It does not say the punishment for sin is death—because whenever you sin, who are you working for? The answer is Satan, and it will be Satan who pays you. It is important to be clear: God made us so that He could love us, and God does not want us to go down. Jesus' incarnation, and His death and resurrection, made a way for human beings to reconnect with God easily, without striving: 'Christ was born into the world He created, but the world did not recognise Him. He came to the people group that were His own, yet they did not receive Him. Nevertheless, whoever does receive Him, believing in His name, has been given the right to become a child of God' (see John 1:10-13). God desires that human beings inherit life, not death.

76 ¶ HE WANTS US CONFORMED TO THE CHARACTER OF HIS SON

The purpose of Father God sending His Son to this world was to create a means of restoring to people their lost identity; and He sent the Holy Spirit to remould their character to become like Christ's. Everything Christ did was for the sake of other people, and to bring joy to the Father. At the same time, Christ Himself experienced great joy and had a love for life. Thus it is the believer's destiny to be changed, by degrees, so that we become like Him: Whenever anyone turns to the Lord a change takes place that can be compared to drawing back the curtains in the morning, and seeing through the window for the first time. As we gaze upon the Lord's glory we begin to reflect Him, and we are increasingly transformed into His image, by the Spirit (see 2 Corinthians 3:18). As Paul explained to the church at Rome, God not only called us but He also predetermined that we should come to resemble Christ, so that He will be the firstborn of the extensive family that God is nurturing (Romans 8:28-29). However, being conformed is a lifelong process: Christ has furnished believers with gifts to help every person grow into spiritual maturity, aiming at the likeness of Christ as the standard, so that we do not remain immature, unsettled and blown about by every wind of doctrine, by human trickery, cunning, and deceitful scheming; but being truthful and loving, we are to grow in every aspect into Christ, who is the head (Ephesians 4:12-15). The maturing of believers is the will of Father God, and the work of the Holy Spirit. Under the old covenant, God's people were one people group with one primary culture, one common history and much the same value system. But now Jesus has opened up the way to God for all people, from every culture and world-view, and all possible experiences of life. Therefore God handles every believer differently, because we are each unique. Every believer is being led toward the same goal of christlikeness, but each is moving from a different starting point. Thus, for example, to the proud person He may teach compassion and humility, whilst for the oppressed person He may build up self-confidence. Our personal journey to maturity has to be unique, and Father God will teach each child the right thing at the right time, using every circumstance to challenge aspects of our life that need changing. For example, people of diverse cultures and customs may disquiet us, but they can be the very agents God uses for shattering our prejudices and dispelling our narrow thinking, when we are willing to be transformed.

Jesus warned His disciples that whilst truly becoming like Him, they could also expect the kind of treatment He received: No disciple is above his teacher, and no slave is above his master, but a disciple can become like his teacher, and a slave like his master. If people slander the head of the house, they will malign the members of his household even more (see Matthew 10:24-25). Just as Jesus' life was undergirded by the love of the Father, our life as believers can be sustained in the same way: 'We know that when He appears, we will be like Him, because we will see Him just as He is' (1 John 3:2). When life is going our way it is easy to display righteous characteristics, but in irritating and unreasonable circumstances it is far more difficult. If believers have godly reactions at such times, this is an indication that they are becoming Christlike.

---

77 ¶ HE WANTS US TO LIVE IN SPIRIT AND TRUTH

Believers are encouraged to live in Spirit and truth. At the creation God gave every human a spirit, a core element of their being which bears the image of their creator God: 'The Lord stretches out the heavens, lays the foundation of the earth, and forms the spirit of person within him' (see Zechariah 12:1). And it is clear that it was God's intention from the beginning that humankind should bear His image: 'God created man in His own image, in the image of God He created him; male and female He created them' (see Genesis 1:27). This spirit, which God first breathed into Adam's nostrils, gives life to our mortal body: If God were to take back to Himself His spirit and withdraw His breath, all flesh would at once perish and humanity would return to dust (see Job 34:14-15). The spirit of humankind longs for God, despite the attractions of the world, the distractions of the soul, and the deceptions of the mind. Through the fall, the mind of humanity was tampered with, in a similar way that a narcotic drug will mess with the mind. The effect of this was to make human beings susceptible to deception, and in particular, deception in respect of the nature of God, and in respect of bearing His image. This deception isolates the human spirit from the human soul, through which we interact with the world and with each other. Consequently, the human spirit feels alone and adrift. Because these feelings are at the core of our being, the soul also detects them as emotions. The soul that is independent of God does all in its power to appease these feelings. However, once the soul of a person is reconnected to God the process begins to reverse: 'He restores my soul, He guides me in the paths of righteousness for His name's sake' (Psalm 23:3). The mind, which is part of the human soul, also undergoes a process of change: You were formerly alienated and hostile in mind, doing evil deeds, but now He has reconciled you through the death of Christ in His physical body, to present you holy, without blemish and beyond reproach before Him (see Colossians 1:21-22). He will progressively remove our deceptions and bring us into all truth. It was always God's intention that His children continually live in His presence, as Jesus did, and therefore life cannot be divided into sacred and secular compartments. Believers may live in Spirit and truth when they are at work, at home with family, in the pub, wherever they are, and in whatever company. The Father is seeking true worshippers, people who trust Him completely without reserve or pretence: 'God is spirit, and those who worship Him must worship in Spirit and in truth' (John 4:24).

78 ¶ HE WANTS US TO BE FREE OF THE WORLD'S DELUSIONS

The Father desires that believers overcome the world system. Shortly before Jesus was to be crucified and then return to Father God, He prayed earnestly for the protection of His followers: 'I have given them Your word and the world has hated them, for they are not of the world any more than I am of the world. My prayer is not that You take them out of the world but that You protect them from the evil one. They are not of the world, even as I am not of it' (John 17:14-16 NIV). Christ Himself overcame the world, with all its enticements, trials and troubles, and He wants believers to experience the same victory. In order to overcome, rather than acting with self-effort, the believer is entreated to surrender to the Spirit, who then provides the resources of God that are appropriate for overcoming in each situation: 'Even though our outer person is wasting away, our inner person is being renewed day by day. For our light and transient trials are bringing forth a weighty and eternal glory for us that is beyond comparison. We do not look at the visible, but at the invisible, for the visible is transient, but the invisible is eternal' (see 2 Corinthians 4:16-18). Jesus warned His disciples that they would have tribulation in the world, but since He has overcome the world, they can take courage (see John 16:32-33). When we have to interact with difficult people, or find ourselves in unpleasant situations, our negative reactions reveal the unhealed wounds of our soul. This revealing can work in our favour when we seek Father God and allow Him to deal with the roots of our pain. As the soul is increasingly healed, believers become less susceptible to their worldly circumstances and less affected by other people's opinions.

The apostle Peter wrote to the early believers who were experiencing persecution, reminding them that Jesus warned His followers this was likely to happen:

Do not be surprised at the trial by fire that you are going through, as though a strange thing were happening to you; but rejoice that you are sharers in the afflictions of Christ, so that when His glory is revealed you will also rejoice with great joy (see 1 Peter 4:12-13). And again Peter praises the believers for continuing to rejoice over their heavenly inheritance, despite suffering many afflictions. He concludes that their trials would work the same way that gold is tested by fire, and serve to authenticate their faith and love for God, which will be rewarded when Christ appears (see 1 Peter 1:4-7). These early Christians experienced supernatural joy even in their persecution, which is evidence that they, like Jesus, were overcoming the delusions of the world.

---

79 ¶ He wants to instigate our destiny

Non-believers may ask themselves 'What would I have to give up to follow God? What sacrifices would I have to make?' But these are essentially false notions because, in fact, we do not lose our autonomy when we become believers. When a person is awakened to his or her inner spiritual man, they realise this is who they really are, and they discover what they have actually wanted to do all along. This awareness gives a strong sense of destiny which, when pursued, gives fulfilment like nothing else. Moreover, our spiritual destiny is designed by the Father to dovetail with others' destiny—there is no threat or competition.

Our destiny in God may or may not have anything to do with earthly success, but as we fulfil the deeds which Father God has prepared for each of us to do, we experience a sense of excitement and satisfaction in our spirit. This is true when we do something with significant results, and equally true when we do something that seems small, because we sense congruence with the eternal realm of God: For we are God's workmanship, created in Christ Jesus for the good works that God prepared beforehand for us to walk in' (Ephesians 2:10). Some suggest that these good works prepared beforehand are written on scrolls which are kept in heaven, and that our reward will be based on whether we have fulfilled what was written on our scroll. This idea is based on Psalm 40:6-8 which the writers of Hebrews consider a description of Jesus' destiny: When Christ came into the world He said, 'Sacrifice and offering You did not desire, but a body You prepared for Me. You took no pleasure in whole burnt offerings and sin offerings. Then I said, "See—as it is written about Me in the scroll—I have come to do Your will, O God"' (Hebrews 10:5-7). In a broad sense, every child of God has a destiny to do the Father's will, as the Holy Spirit leads us.

The resurrected Jesus intercepted Saul (whom He renamed Paul) whilst he was on his way to arrest Christians. But rather than condemning him, He revealed his destiny to him: 'I have appeared to you for the purpose of appointing you a minister and a witness both to me, and to the things that I will reveal to you. I will rescue you from your own people, and from the Gentiles to whom I am sending you, to open their eyes so that they turn from darkness to light, and from the power of Satan to God, receiving forgiveness of sins and an inheritance with those sanctified through faith in Me' (Acts 26:16-18). Saul always wanted to serve God, but his zeal was misplaced until Christ opened his eyes to the truth. Father God wants us to know that He has put our most precious dreams within us, and He wants us to be awakened to them.

---

80 ¶ HE WILL NOT OVERRIDE THE HUMAN WILL

When God created humankind He gave us free will. He did not want to make us like robots that automatically do what He wants. He also did not want us to be like slaves who know it is pointless to resist. Free will is a precious gift to us, and God treats our free will as though it is a sacred thing. Thus, He will never violate human free will, and even though He desperately wants us to love Him, He will not force us. The bridegroom urges the daughters of Jerusalem: 'Do not arouse or awaken love until it so desires' (see Song of Solomon 2:7) and God applies this principle to Himself. We see Jesus respecting people's free will when they come to Him for prayer. He asks a blind man: 'What do you want Me to do for you?' (Luke 18:41) even though it might seem obvious that he would wish to regain his sight. But the principle is important—Jesus is engaging the person's will. Not everybody has their physical healing as their highest priority.

Although some people have had their will damaged, maybe because in childhood they were dominated, or their choices were restrained, nevertheless nothing can destroy their free will when it comes to choosing to turn to God. There is a story in Mark's gospel about a man who was possessed by about two thousand demons. This man was in a terrible state, but when Jesus got out of the boat he immediately came to meet Him. The man was living in the graveyard, and nobody was able to restrain him, although they had tried using shackles and chains, but each time he had torn them off and broken them to pieces, being unnaturally strong. Day and night he was constantly screaming in the graveyard or in the mountains, and he would slash himself with stones. When he saw Jesus from a distance, he ran to Him and bowed down before Him (see Mark 5:2-6). This man was being drawn towards Jesus and as he responded he was rewarded with deliverance and healing.

In Luke 23 we find an account of the two criminals who were crucified with Jesus, one on each side, with Jesus in the middle: 'One of the criminals hanging there kept reviling Him, saying, "You are supposed to be the Christ, so save Yourself and us!" But the other criminal rebuked him saying, "Don't you fear God? We've all been condemned to the same punishment, and we deserve it because of what we did; but this man hasn't done anything wrong." Then turning to Jesus he said, "Jesus, remember me when You come into Your kingdom!" And Jesus replied, "I tell you the truth, today you shall be with Me in Paradise.'" (see Luke 23:39-43). This story shows that even if somebody has made bad choices all their life, that does not prevent them choosing to turn to God, even at the last minute. God has placed salvation within the reach of everyone, simply through making the decision to trust Jesus.

Paul tells the Corinthian believers, 'You are not your own for you have been bought with a price' (see 1 Corinthians 6:19-20), nevertheless God does not take our free will from us. We have the option of submitting our will to the will of God, or refusing. Every command God makes to us is an appeal to the will; at the same time He is the one who gives us the desire to choose appropriately, 'lest anyone should boast' (Ephesians 2:9).

11

———

LIVING AS BELOVED CHILDREN

81. We can freely appropriate God's grace
82. We can love one another as God loved us first
83. We are able to participate in God's forgiveness
84. We are able to love our enemies
85. We can live in freedom
86. We are emissaries for His purposes on earth
87. We are able to trust in His provision
88. We are able to commune with the Father

---

81 ¶ We can freely appropriate God's grace

When believers commune with God they have access to His grace. Some religious groups try to deny the deity of Jesus by using an incorrect definition of grace, as 'unmerited favour'. Their skewed argument goes like this: in John's gospel it states Jesus was full of grace and truth (see John 1:14), therefore Jesus was full of unmerited favour, so, they suggest, since He did not merit favour, He was merely a man. But this is based on a huge error. The term 'unmerited favour' describes the fact that human beings have not earned God's grace by being good, but it is not a definition of grace. Grace is actually the provision of spiritual resources which we need in order to fulfil the will of God. Grace thus enables us to continue the work of Christ on earth, and to react to situations as Christ would. Whenever we agree to something that God is prompting us to do (or to stop doing), we qualify for His grace. And His grace is perfected in direct proportion to our weakness. Conversely, whenever we try to do things without Him we are acting in our human strength, which can only bring a human result.

Grace is part of the inheritance bestowed on us by God while we are in this earthly life. We are encouraged to be good stewards of the 'manifold grace of God' (see 1 Peter 4:10). Our pride says, 'I can do this without any help', but when we acknowledge our need of God we instantly qualify for grace (see 1 Peter 5:5-6 and James 4:6-7). The early Christians understood this, and were quite excited about it. Paul signs off all his letters by wishing his readers the grace of God. This was not simply a convention of those times, as we might end a letter with 'Yours faithfully' today; Paul's sign-off is a blessing, and it is a reminder that this new covenant operates through God's heavenly resources, not through human effort to please God: 'We have conducted ourselves in the world, and especially in our relations with you, with integrity and godly sincerity. We have done so, relying not on worldly wisdom but on God's grace' (2 Corinthians 1:12 NIV).

In another sense, grace can be considered to be God's provision that is extended to all humanity, and the earth, since He created and sustains life, and causes 'His sun to rise on the evil and the good, and sends rain on the righteous and unrighteous' (see Matthew 5:45). In addition, it is also the grace of God that everybody has a human spirit which longs for Him. When anyone receives salvation through the working of His grace, it activates the human spirit, which begins the restoration of the soul, by awakening us to the truth, and removing our deceptions. All this is achieved by the grace of God.

---

82 ¶ We can love one another as God loved us first

Father God enables believers to love as He loves. The well-known bible passage on love, which is so often read at weddings, actually describes the qualities of God's own love: 'Love is patient, love is kind. It does not envy, it does not boast, it is not proud. It does not dishonour others, it is not self-seeking, it is not easily angered, it keeps no record of wrongs. Love does not delight in evil but rejoices with the truth. It always protects, always trusts, always hopes, always perseveres. Love never fails' (1 Corinthians 13:4-8 NIV).

The apostle John fully understood the extent of God's love towards him, describing himself as 'the disciple whom Jesus loved'. In his letter he explains that the origin of love is God Himself: 'Beloved, love one another, for love is from God. Everyone who loves is born of God and knows God. Whoever does not love does not know God, because God is love' (1 John 4:7-8). In the Greek language of the New Testament there are several different words for 'love'. When Jesus expresses His desire that we would love one another, even as He has loved us, the Greek word used is 'agape'. Jesus tells His followers: 'By this all men will know that you are My disciples, if you have love for one another' (John 13:35). Many people love one another, but in this case, there is meant to be a distinctive—something that sets the followers of Jesus apart. There are not many definitive instructions in the new covenant, but to love the Lord our God with all our heart, mind, soul and strength, and to love our neighbour as ourselves, is clearly stated. These words appear as commandments. Jesus said: 'If you love Me you will keep My commandments' (John 14:15). The thing that compels believers to fulfil these commandments is their love for Christ. The commands seem simple, but in practice our hearts cannot switch on the love by themselves. We need supernatural help because we can so easily get irritated, even by those we care about. Clearly, we need God's own love, not our fallen, self-centred love, which only operates when reciprocated. As we receive God's love for ourselves, this same love enables us to love others: 'We love because He first loved us. If a person says he loves God but hates his brother, he is a liar. For if he does not love his brother, whom he has seen, he cannot love God, whom he has not seen' (1 John 4:19-20). Indeed, the evidence that we are reciprocating God's love is our change of heart towards other people.

While Jesus' second commandment is to 'love your neighbour as you love yourself' (Mark 12:31), there are many people who, for a variety of reasons, do not love themselves. This can cause difficulties in relationships, and even doubts that God could love them. But John explains: 'This is love, not that we loved God, but that He loved us and sent His Son as an atoning sacrifice for our sins. Beloved, since God so loved us we also ought to love one another. No one has ever seen God, but if we love one another, God abides in us and His love has reached its goal in us' (1 John 4:10-11). When we live in awareness of the love God has for us, this heals the heart and enables us to love others.

---

83 ¶ WE ARE ABLE TO PARTICIPATE IN GOD'S FORGIVENESS

God has provided forgiveness for believers, and desires them to forgive others. We are told: 'Death reigned from the time of Adam until the time of Moses' (Romans 5:14). This suggests something happened at the time of Moses to reduce death's power. The Israelites were slaves in Egypt. Ten times Moses went to Pharaoh asking him to let God's people go, but each time he refused. Finally, God sent the destroyer to kill the firstborn in every household; but God told the Israelites if they were to kill a lamb and sprinkle its blood on their doorposts, the destroyer would pass over them without harm. Thus the lamb would die instead of the Jewish people. This was the change in the time of Moses— death did not reign any more, it was brought under control to some degree by substitutional death. Throughout the time of the old covenant, animals were killed as blood sacrifices to substitute for the punishment due to people who had sinned. Most frequently these animals were lambs. When Jesus first appeared in public, John the Baptist cried out, 'Behold the Lamb of God who takes away the sin of the world' (John 1:29). This was Jesus' mandate—He came to save us from our sins (see Matthew 1:21). Satan gains rights over humans when we sin—he is after our blood. However, when anyone receives God's forgiveness, those rights are removed. It was necessary for Jesus to shed His blood in order to secure forgiveness on behalf of humankind. This is because one of the laws of Satan's world system is, 'without the shedding of blood there is no forgiveness' (see Hebrews 9:22). As Jesus explained at the last supper, 'This is My blood of the new covenant, which is poured out for many for the forgiveness of sins' (Matthew 26:28).

As believers, our access to this new life with Jesus comes together with receiving forgiveness for our own sins direct from God Himself. As a consequence, we no longer get the wages of our sin, which is death, but God gives us fullness of life instead. And our heavenly Father desires us to be on the side of life, not death. Therefore, He also wants us to cooperate with Him by being willing to forgive others. Because forgiveness removes Satan's rights, it can sometimes open the way for people to believe in Jesus. This happened to the centurion and other men from the crucifixion unit, who nailed Jesus to the cross: Jesus prayed, 'Father forgive them for they don't know what they do'. Soon afterwards these hardened Roman executioners said: 'Truly this man was the Son of God' (see Matthew 27:54). God's forgiveness made something change in those men. Stephen was the first follower of Jesus to be killed for his faith—the crowd stoned him to death. And a man called Saul stood by, watching, while he guarded the coats of the people who were throwing the stones. Stephen prayed, 'Lord, do not hold this sin against them' (see Acts 7:60). Later, Saul had a dramatic encounter with Jesus on the road to Damascus, and became a changed man.

God's forgiveness destroys Satan's work. Scripture explains, 'the weapons of our warfare are not of the flesh, but are empowered by God for tearing down strongholds' (2 Corinthians 10:4), and forgiveness is one such weapon. God gives His children revelation of this forgiveness, and He enjoins them to be agents of forgiveness, as the Holy Spirit leads them: 'Jesus said, "Peace be with you! As the Father has sent Me, I am sending you." And with that He breathed on them and said, "Receive the Holy Spirit. If you forgive anyone's sins, their sins are forgiven; if you retain anyone's sins, they are retained"' (John 20:21-23). This is a formidable responsibility, and believers should ask themselves if they are comfortable with someone remaining unforgiven as a result of their decision. If however believers decide to forgive, the person concerned will have that sin erased forever. In this respect we become co-workers with God.

When believers are given the courage to confess their sins to one another, as the Holy Spirit leads them, this creates a godly trust that does not exist in any other group of people: 'If we walk in the light as He is in the light, we have fellowship with one another, and the blood of Jesus His Son cleanses us from all sin. If we say that we have no sin, we deceive ourselves and the truth is not in us. If we confess our sins, He is faithful and just and will forgive us our sins and cleanse us from all falsehood' (1 John 1:7-9). However, Satan, the accuser of the brethren, can often make people feel ashamed or embarrassed about things that have happened, even when they are not responsible, or when the Holy Spirit is not convicting them. When God gives believers the grace to be open with one another, and they are prompted by the Holy Spirit, being transparent can actually become a safeguard, and it is also true that, 'Anyone who believes in Him will never be put to shame' (Romans 10:11). Together we can experience God's forgiveness.

---

84 ¶ WE ARE ABLE TO LOVE OUR ENEMIES

The Father intends us to love our enemies, as Jesus explained, "You have heard it said, 'Love your neighbour and hate your enemy.' But I say love your enemies and pray for those who persecute you, so you will be sons of your Father in heaven. He causes His sun to rise on the evil and the good, and sends rain on the just and the unjust. If you love those who love you, will you be rewarded? Tax collectors even do that. If you only greet your family, is that impressive? Heathens do that. Be perfect as your heavenly Father is perfect" (Matthew 5:43-48). If ever we had any delusions that we could love without help from God, this instruction of Jesus shows it is impossible. The bible describes God's supernatural love, which we are able to draw upon: 'love is patient, love is kind. It does not envy, it does not boast, it is not proud. It does not dishonour others, it is not self-seeking, it is not easily angered, it keeps no record of wrongs...' (1 Corinthians 13:4-5 NIV). When we are left to our own devices, we are often impatient, sometimes unkind, we have been known to envy and boast, and we can be proud. We have surely dishonoured others and sought our own interests, as well as becoming angry. We certainly remember bad things people have done to us. If we were to attempt to act according to the definition of love found in 1 Corinthians by 'trying harder' that would be mere religion, behaviour control, acting superficially to gain approval or to feel good about ourselves. Jesus is looking for our willingness to surrender to His will, and as we do so His grace will enable us to love our enemies as He loves them. God's encouragement in the scripture to, 'be perfect, as your heavenly Father is perfect', (Matthew 5:48) deliberately sets the bar too high for any human effort to attain.

God sees us as we can be, and this is how He wants us to view our enemies: 'But God demonstrates His own love toward us, in that while we were yet sinners, Christ died for us' (Romans 5:8). God's nature is love, kindness and mercy. He will not change His nature, even in relation to those whose nature is self-centred and hateful—He will persist in loving them, just as He persisted in loving us until we responded and were changed. His hope is that we align ourselves with His desire that none perish, even those whose depravity we despise, since we do not focus on their behaviour, but on God's love for them.

Often people do not understand who their enemies are. Jesus said: 'How can Satan cast out Satan? If a kingdom is divided against itself, that kingdom cannot stand' (Mark 3:23-24). In the world system, people believe they are unconnected to others who are not in the same grouping. For example, Fascists thought they had nothing in common with Communists; the Hutu tribe thought they had nothing in common with the Tutsi tribe. If we liken each group to a cog inside a watch, they seem unconnected until we look closely at the mechanism, where it is clear that the movement of each cog affects all the others. Although a kingdom divided against itself cannot stand, they do stand because they are not really divided. Satan wants them to think they are divided, and thus he maintains the deception that they are enemies. The kingdom of this world is under Satan's control, but the kingdom of God is an entirely different entity. Yet the same principle is at work; different Christian groupings are connected whether they realise it or not. Believers will not be aware of this when their differentiation of friend and enemy depends on people holding the same doctrines. It is only when believers are in the Spirit that they can truly see who their friends and enemies are—both of whom we are called to love.

---

85 ¶ WE CAN LIVE IN FREEDOM

The Father intends believers to live in their freedom, enabled by the Holy Spirit: 'Now the Lord is the Spirit, and where the Spirit of the Lord is, there is freedom' (2

Corinthians 3:17). If a person adheres to an external ethical code of behaviour, such as the Mosaic Law, they feel obliged or compelled to conform to it. However, when believers are internally led by the Holy Spirit they become free from conflicting obligations, and this includes trying to gain acceptance or approval from other people, especially from religious authority figures. Jesus identified the cause of the Pharisees' unbelief. He said to them, 'You search the scriptures because you suppose in them you will have eternal life, yet they testify about Me. But you refuse to come to Me to have life. I do not accept glory from people, but I know you do not have the love of God in you. I have come in My Father's name and you do not accept Me; but if someone else comes in his own name, you will accept him. How can you believe when you accept glory from one another but do not seek the glory that comes from the only God?' (John 5:39-44).

Jesus did not change His behaviour according to the company He was with, because He was completely secure in His identity, and was continuously led by the Spirit. He would not entrust Himself to anyone because He was well aware of human nature, and He had no need to be told about anyone because He knew what was in each person (see John 2:24-25). Whilst the Pharisees saw themselves as superior and kept themselves separate from their inferiors, Jesus associated with the lowly and those who were despised by society, outcasts and rejects: 'While Jesus was having dinner at Levi's house, many tax collectors and sinners were eating with Him and his disciples, for many of them followed Him' (Mark 2:15). Jesus was unaffected by flattery and insults alike, because He knew the immutable source of His affirmation and approval was His heavenly Father: 'All good and perfect gifts are from above, given by the Father of lights, who does not change like shifting shadows' (James 1:17). In our case also it is true to say that God could not love us more, and He will not love us less, regardless of our religious performance. This knowledge, once received by revelation, not only brings freedom from trying to win God's approval, but can also bring freedom from fear of man's disapproval: 'For freedom Christ has set us free, so persevere and do not be subject again to a yoke of slavery. I, Paul, warn you, if you receive circumcision, Christ will be no benefit to you. And I repeat, every man who receives circumcision is under obligation to keep the entire Law. You are severed from Christ by seeking to be justified by Law; you have forfeited grace' (Galatians 5:1-4). The slavery Paul warns about here relates to believers who wanted to avoid criticism by some religious men who told them they needed to be circumcised in order to be saved. Paul was angry about this deception and restated the truth in no uncertain terms: 'If anyone preaches a gospel different from the one you received, let him be accursed. I am not seeking to please man, but God. If I were still trying to seek favour with man, I would not be a servant of Christ.' (see

Galatians 1:9-10). Our religious performance has no value to God because if we return to trying to fulfil religious obligations it shows we have forgotten we are His beloved children. But even when believers do feel sure of God's love and approval they can be distracted by the natural desire to be part of a human 'in crowd'. Such groups derive their attractiveness from the very fact that outsiders are excluded. The apostle Paul makes this point in his letter: 'They eagerly seek you, not commendably, but they wish to shut you out so that you will seek them' (Galatians 4:17 NASB). Enduring rejection can often be the price believers pay for refusing to compromise their convictions, and this is not easy because human instinct recoils from rejection: 'Many believed in Jesus, even among the rulers, but because they feared the Pharisees they would not confess it openly, in case they were cast out of the synagogue. For they loved the praise of men more than the praise of God' (John 12:42-43). However, through God's grace believers can live free from the need of human approval, acceptance and accolade.

---

86 ¶ We are emissaries for His purposes on earth

Jesus explained that believers will continue the work of the Father on earth: 'Whoever believes in Me will do the works I have been doing, and they will do even greater things, because I am going to the Father' (John

14:12). Although Jesus was fully God He would regularly spend time alone in prayer to His Father. When He taught the disciples to pray He was not giving them a format of words to recite, on the contrary, He warned them not to pray long repetitive prayers: 'When you pray do not use meaningless repetition as the Gentiles do, for they imagine they will be heard for their many words. Do not be like them, for your Father knows what you need before you ask Him' (Matthew 6:7-8). The way Jesus prayed was based on the absolute certainty that God is a good and loving Father: 'Even though you are bad, you know how to give good gifts to your children. How much more will your Father in heaven give good things to those who ask Him!' (Matthew 7:11). One of the entreaties in The Lord's Prayer is, 'Your will be done'. These words were never intended to be recited by rote, but the idea is that we listen to the Holy Spirit, then align our prayers with His will. Central to this idea is the concept of fasting. Jesus was alluding to Himself when He told His disciples that the wedding guests cannot mourn while the bridegroom is still with them, but when the bridegroom has been taken from them, then they would fast (see Matthew 9:15), because they would long to have union with Him again. When believers are aware of the Holy Spirit, however, they know that the Lord is in fact with them all the time. Fasting now, therefore, is refusing to be ruled by our body and its clamouring demands; and by our human, soulish thinking, which stops us hearing from God. Thus, when the early church began assigning tasks to people, they fasted in order to subjugate their own opinions and preferences to the Holy Spirit, enabling them to discern God's choice (see Acts 13:1-2).

There are many needs and issues that could grab our attention, but when we pray in the will of the Father we shall see answers to our prayers: 'This is how confident we are as we approach Him: if we ask anything according to His will, He hears us, and if we know He hears whenever we ask, we know we receive the requests we have asked for' (1 John 5:14-15).

When God put humankind on the earth He gave us responsibility to manage all the earth's resources. He told Adam and Eve to populate the earth, to keep it in good order, and to rule over the living creatures (see Genesis 1:28). 'The heavens are the heavens of the Lord, but the earth He has given to the sons of men' (Psalm 115:16 NASB). It was His intention that we steward the earth wisely. But since humanity has habitually acted independently from God, we have failed in this task enormously. Yet God has always revealed His wishes to individuals who are His friends, who align themselves with His will and pray, as the prophet explains: 'Surely the Lord God does nothing unless He reveals His secret counsel to His servants the prophets' (Amos 3:7). Thus, God acts on earth in response to people's prayers. Because Christianity is not a fatalistic religion, we cannot simply attribute things that happen on earth to the perfect will of our God: 'We know that we are children of God, yet the entire world lies in the power of the evil one. We also know that the Son of God has given us discernment...' (1 John 5:19-20). Some texts in the bible refer to future events that are not pleasing to God, but these are warnings, or prophetic indicators. He did not want Israel to have a king, for example, but He allowed it because His people demanded it. A further example is where the bible predicts increased wars, famines and earthquakes (see Matthew 24:7) before Christ returns. However, since we know God does not want suffering it is unlikely the Holy Spirit will lead believers to pray for such disasters. Through the Spirit-led prayers of His followers which, by definition, are in alignment with the 'good, pleasing and perfect' will of God (see Romans 12:2), He can intervene in wretched human situations, and Satan's hurtful strategies can be averted. In this way believers act as emissaries for the Father's purposes on the earth.

---

87 ¶ We are able to trust in His provision

Jesus explained to His followers that Father God is generous, and will provide for His children: 'Do not be anxious about your life, what you will eat and drink, or what you will wear. Life is not just food, and the body is not just clothing. The birds of the air make no effort to grow food to eat, yet your heavenly Father feeds them, and you are worth far more than them. And worrying cannot add one extra hour to your life. Why worry about clothes? The most beautiful flowers grow effortlessly, yet even the clothing of kings does not equal their splendour. If God clothes the fields with flowers He will provide clothing for you. You do not need to concern yourselves with these things, for your heavenly Father knows what you need. But seek first His kingdom and His righteousness, and all these other things will be given too' (see Matthew 6:25-33).

Therefore we ourselves can venture to be generous, and we do not need to accumulate riches on earth, because our Father will care for us. Besides this, our true treasure is in heaven and we are aware that our time on earth is transient, but our life in heaven is everlasting. As Jesus said: 'Do not store up for treasure for yourself on earth, where moths and rust can spoil them, and where thieves break in and steal them. Rather, store up treasures for yourself in heaven, out of harm's way. For where your treasure is, there your heart will also be' (see Matthew 6:19-21).

Father God wants His children to be free from the deceptions of money, as Jesus explained, nobody can serve God and mammon. Money, or mammon, tells us 'you need me to be safe'. Logically, if we give money away we will lose something, but God tells us we will gain something. Paul encourages believers to help the needy, reminding them that Jesus Himself said, 'It is more blessed to give than to receive' (see Acts 20:35). God defies logic, but when we give our money generously this can break the power it has over us. However, when we give we should be led by the Holy Spirit and motivated by love, not by duty. We must never think of our giving as paying our dues to God so that He will do something for us in return. He is the source of all we have, and therefore He can never be indebted to anyone. But God wants His children to have generous hearts because this reflects His own kindness and generosity.

As Paul understood God to be his provider, he experienced freedom from the shifting fortunes of the world: 'I have learned to be content whatever my circumstances. I have experienced need, and abundance. I find contentment in every situation, whether full or hungry, having plenty or in want. I do this through the One who strengthens me' (see Philippians 4:11-13). Paul was called to serve God and he walked in the Spirit, yet he and the early believers suffered the loss of their material possessions (see Hebrews 10:34). This clearly demonstrates that believers' prosperity is not an indicator of their godliness. But when believers 'seek first the Kingdom of God' they increasingly understand that they have a better and more permanent treasure in heaven. This has the effect of liberating them from the 'deceptiveness of riches' and helps them trust in Jesus' promise that Father God will meet the needs of His children, as appropriate for their best interests. Therefore God might not provide what they demand if it is likely to hinder their spiritual development, because

He also disciplines the children He loves in order to make them holy (see Hebrews 12:5-11).

---

88 ¶ We are able to commune with the Father

Believers are encouraged to spend time with the Father: 'Draw near to God and He will draw near to you' (James 4:8). It is this intimacy with Him that also enables believers to discern His perfect will: 'Live as children of light (the fruit of light consists of all goodness, righteousness and truth) and find out what pleases the Lord' (Ephesians 5:8-10). This advises that we stay close to God, telling Him our concerns, and listening for His voice. Jesus defined friendship as telling each other our thoughts and desires, saying 'I have called you friends, for everything I have heard from My Father I have made known to you' (John 15:15). We are friends of God as we commune with Him. It is during this communion that the believer begins to understand how God feels and thinks about things. Because believers know they are dearly loved, they feel safe to tell the Father everything—their secrets, their opinions, their fears, and things about themselves they would be too embarrassed to tell other people. When believers give Him their honesty, He will exchange it for His truth.

Being in His presence is also enjoyable, both for believers and for Father God, as John described: 'We have told you what we have seen and heard, so that you will have fellowship with us. And our fellowship is also with the Father and with His Son, Jesus Christ. We are writing this so that our joy may be complete' (1 John 1:3-4). The Greek word used for fellowship is 'koinonia' which describes a close communion. This intimacy with God is satisfying because it fulfils a human need that cannot be met by anything else. For believers, God continuously makes Himself present. However, when we live soulishly we can lose our awareness of Him. This is the reason He asks us to put our soulish activities on hold in order to make ourselves present to Him: 'When you pray, go away by yourself, shut the door behind you, and pray to your Father in private. Then your Father, who sees everything, will reward you' (Matthew 6:6).

12

OUR ETERNAL IDENTITY

89. We are loved by the I AM
90. We are His prized possession
91. We are no longer orphans
92. We have inherited eternal life
93. We are made holy and blameless
94. We have an eternal place with God
95. We shall be made new
96. We embody God's ultimate plans

89 ¶ WE ARE LOVED BY THE I AM

God identifies Himself with the name 'I AM'. The moment He first chooses to do this is significant. The Israelites had been enslaved to the Egyptians for four hundred years, and Moses, although brought up by Pharaoh's daughter, had spent forty years hiding from the Egyptian authorities. He was in the wilderness one day and noticed a bush that was on fire, but was not burning up. He approached, and from within the bush, the voice of God told him he had been commissioned to bring the Israelites out of their slavery in Egypt. But Moses was not sure people would take him seriously. He said to God, 'If I go to the Israelites and tell them that the God of their fathers has sent me to them, and they ask me what is his name, what shall I say?' God replied, 'I AM who I AM. This is what you are to say to the Israelites—I AM has sent me to you' (see Exodus 3:13-14). God also said to Moses: 'Tell the sons of Israel that the Lord, the God of your fathers, the God of Abraham, the God of Isaac, and the God of Jacob, has sent me to you. This is My name forever, and this is My memorial-name to all generations. Gather the elders of Israel and tell them, "The Lord, the God of your fathers, the God of Abraham, Isaac and Jacob, has appeared to me, saying, 'I am concerned about you and what has been done to you in Egypt, so I will bring you out of the affliction of Egypt to a land flowing with milk and honey"' (see Exodus 3:15-17). When God reveals His eternal name, this is coupled with the promise that He will rescue His people from the bondage of Egypt. Thus the Exodus points forward to the time when Jesus would come in the flesh to rescue humanity from bondage to the kingdom of this world. The revealing of God's eternal name shows God's purpose from the beginning, which was to redeem those who believe.

The Exodus itself began with each Hebrew family slaughtering a lamb and putting its blood over their door frame, in order that the angel of death would pass over their household without harm. Centuries later, John the Baptist revealed Jesus as 'the Lamb of God who takes away the sins of the world'. However, Christ not only rescues us from slavery to the darkness of this world, but He also brings us into His presence for eternity. This is how Peter describes Christ, as 'the One who called you out of darkness into His marvellous light' (1 Peter 2:9).

In Exodus 3 God not only reveals His identity as I AM, but also through His memorial-name: 'The God of Abraham, the God of Isaac and the God of Jacob.' These three patriarchs are analogous of the Trinity. God the Father identifies Himself through Abraham, who was prophetically called the 'father of all nations'. Jesus, the Son of God, identifies Himself through Isaac, the promised beloved son, who was offered as a sacrifice. The Holy Spirit identifies Himself through Jacob. The Hebrew meaning of the name Jacob is 'one who supplants'. When she was pregnant, Jacob's mother was told by God that she would give birth to twins, but the elder would serve the younger (see Genesis 25:23-24). Jacob's elder brother relinquished his birthright to Jacob in exchange for food (see Genesis 25:29-34). When the twins' father was dying, their mother arranged for Jacob to receive the father's blessing instead of his elder brother (see Genesis 27:6-32). Thus Jacob supplanted, or displaced, his older brother's ascendency. This represents the work of the Holy Spirit, who wishes to supplant the dominance of the natural, fleshly nature within the believer: '...walk by the Spirit, and you will not carry out the desire of the flesh. For the flesh sets its desire against the Spirit, and the Spirit against the flesh; for these are in opposition to one another' (Galatians 5:16-17 NASB).

In addition, God's name 'I AM' is a declaration that the Trinity is unaffected by time—He always was, He always will be, and He will never change. As the New Testament writers state, 'Jesus Christ is the same yesterday and today and forever' (Hebrews 13:8) and 'Every good and perfect gift is from above, coming down from the Father of light, who does not change like shifting shadows' (James 1:17). The bible relates an instance when Jesus referred to Himself as 'I AM', and the religious authorities interpreted this as Jesus declaring Himself to be God. They were enraged, and intended to stone Him to death for blasphemy: Jesus said to them, 'I tell you the truth, before Abraham came to be, I AM.' Therefore they picked up stones to throw at Him, but Jesus hid Himself and went out of the temple (John 8:58-59).

God has chosen to make us the object of His love for eternity; all persons of the Trinity are involved in preparing us to be with Him forever: 'If anyone professes that Jesus is the Son of God, God abides in him and he in God. Thus we discern and trust in the love God has for us. God is love and anyone who abides in love abides in God, and God abides in him. Through this, love is perfected among us so that we will have confidence in the day of judgment, because as He is, so are we in this world' (1 John 4:15-17). We are loved, now and forever, by the I AM.

---

90 ¶ We are His prized possession

The Father lovingly treats the 'ekklesia' of believers as His own possession, which He has given to Christ: 'My sheep listen to My voice, I know them, and they follow Me; I give them eternal life and they will never perish; and no one will snatch them out of My hand. My Father, who has given them to Me, is all powerful, and no one is able to snatch them out of the Father's hand' (John 10:27-30). Christ further explains that all who come to Him will be His forever: 'Everyone the Father gives Me will come to Me, and those who come to Me I will never cast out. I have not come down from heaven to do My own will, but the will of Him who sent Me. It is His will that I lose no one He has given Me, but raise them up on the last day' (John 6:37-39). Also, when believers are deeply aware that they are treasured by God, this motivates them to live their lives to please Him: 'Christ gave Himself for us, to redeem us from all sin and to purify for Himself a people that are His very own, eager to do what is good' (Titus 2:13-14). It is reassuring for believers to know they are God's treasured possession, and He will therefore never give up on them.

---

91 ¶ We are no longer orphans

Believers are able to experience the perfect spiritual parenting of Father God, regardless of the quality of parenting received from their natural parents. Even King David expresses his longing to be loved in this way by God: 'Do not turn Your back on me, do not reject Your servant in anger; You have always been my help; do not leave me or abandon me, O God of my salvation! For my father and my mother have forsaken me, but the Lord will take me in' (Psalm 27:9-10). Because He loved us first, the Father has already given His promise never to abandon us: 'Can a mother forget the baby at her breast and have no compassion on the child she has borne? Though she may forget, I will not forget you!' (Isaiah 49:15). The entire scheme of Christ coming to rescue us was to fulfil the Father's long-term desire: 'God decided in advance to adopt us into His own family, by bringing us to Himself through Jesus Christ. This is what He wanted, and it gave Him great pleasure' (see Ephesians 1:5 NLT).

As babies, we are all born with legitimate needs, and we are instinctively aware of who should meet those needs. We might expect our human need for identity, protection and provision to be met by our earthly father; our need for companionship and communication to be met by our siblings and friends; and our need for nurture, comfort and teaching to be met by our mother. If those needs are not met in childhood, when we become adults we will still be seeking what we need, looking for earthly substitute parents who will give us love and affirmation. But this search can last a whole lifetime yet be unsuccessful, driving us to go from one person to the next, hoping and being disappointed, over and over again. This pattern can influence all our relationships, especially marriage. It is true to say that human approval, even when it comes from fellow believers, will never bring lasting fulfilment. Besides, when people gain their identity from the nice things other people say about them this can be a source of insecurity, since human praise, as well as criticism, is soulish and fickle.

People who have a father who truly loves them have a great benefit in life because fathers have the ability to unlock the treasures of their children's hearts. Nevertheless, much human tragedy stems from the fact that all human beings are born as spiritual orphans. Only our heavenly Father can provide and establish true spiritual identity and affirmation. And when believers know God as their loving Father, this opens the way to unlock their true self. Father God's nurture and approval changes everything—it makes us immune to wanting celebrity status, immune to insults, immune to flattery. We are no longer orphans, but we are safe in the Father's loving arms.

---

92 ¶ We have inherited eternal life

Death is the one experience guaranteed to every human being, but because it is not known what that will be like, or indeed whether there will be any existence after our human body expires, there is fear and speculation. There are a few people who claim to have died and returned to life, but their stories are inconclusive; some people believe death simply brings an end to our existence, but when it comes to their own death, can they be certain? There is only one actual source of knowledge—Christ, who died and was raised from the dead. Ultimately, anyone who turns to Him, even to enquire about the end of their own life, will be accepted by Him. 'God Himself has testified that He has given us eternal life, and this life is in His Son. Anyone who has the Son has the life' (see 1 John 5:11-12).

We are told that even before Christ's incarnation, people who had faith in God's promises regarded themselves as strangers and exiles in this world. They longed for a better, heavenly homeland, and God prepared a city for them to live in (see Hebrews 11:13-16). For believers, the certain knowledge that we will reside in a heavenly eternal place with the Father changes our attitude to this life, and gives courage to those facing death. The apostle Paul was in a Roman prison and in danger of being put to death when he wrote: 'I trust that my life will bring honour to Christ, whether I live or whether I die. For I live for Christ, but dying I gain Christ. If I continue to live I can do more fruitful work for Christ, yet I long to go and be with Him, which would be far better for me' (see Philippians 1:20-23). Christ's followers are encouraged to keep an eternal perspective during their time on earth, being always aware that they are sojourners passing through: 'The world is passing away, along with all its enticements and pleasures, but whoever does the will of God lives forever' (1 John 2:17). And Jesus urges His disciples to keep this perspective even in respect of their spiritual ministry: 'Do not rejoice that the spirits are subject to you, but rejoice that your names have been recorded in heaven' (Luke 10:20). Eternal life is the believer's sure inheritance.

93 ¶ WE ARE MADE HOLY AND BLAMELESS

Believers are forgiven, and therefore considered blameless. At the same time, they are undergoing a process of being made holy. The word 'holy' is often misunderstood as meaning 'good' or even 'super-good'. In the Old Testament, however, we read that fire-pans, forks and shovels that were used in the tabernacle were called holy (see Ezra 8:28, Numbers 7:1). But, of course, these items are neutral in the moral sense. What being holy really means is to be owned by God, to be set apart for Him alone. In the New Testament letters, Paul often refers to believers as 'holy ones', or in some bible translations, 'saints' (Greek: hagios). This alludes to the fact that we are no longer our own, but have been bought with a price (see 1 Corinthians 6:19-20). There may well have been certain individuals who did great exploits of faith, who have been canonised, but all children of God are set apart for Him, that is to say, 'saints' or 'holy ones'. Believers are already fully blameless, but we are also being made holy as we surrender further areas of our lives to God, and are thus being prepared to be used for His purposes: 'For by one sacrifice He has made perfect forever those who are being made holy' (Hebrews 10:14). This can be compared to a person who buys a house, thus it belongs to him, but then he makes it 'his own' as he renovates every room in turn.

---

94 ¶ WE HAVE AN ETERNAL PLACE WITH GOD

Christ informs believers that He has prepared a place for them in His Father's home, both when they die and for the age to come: 'Do not let your heart be troubled. You trust in God; trust also in Me. In My Father's house there are many dwelling places; if that were not the case, would I have told you that I am going there to prepare a place for you? And if I go and prepare a place for you, I will come again and take you to be with Me, so that where I am, there you may be also' (John 14:1-3 Mounce). These words of Jesus have been a great comfort to many people as they approach death. Because of Jesus' words, many like to describe the transition from this life to the next as a 'homecoming'. And believers understand that their heavenly home is both welcoming and personalised for each of the Father's children. Paul referred to our mortal bodies as a temporary 'tent', which is wrapped around our eternal inner being, giving us a means of interfacing with this world and other people: 'For while we remain in this tent, we groan and are burdened, not because we wish to be unclothed, but instead to be clothed with our heavenly dwelling, so that what is mortal may be swallowed up by life' (2 Corinthians 5:4-8). Even in the last hours of His life, Jesus gave this promise to the thief who was being crucified next to Him, who set his hope in Christ during his last moments. As Jesus made abundantly clear in His parable of the 'prodigal son,' it was always Father God's longing for lost humanity to return to His house. He sent His only begotten Son to do all that was needed to make this possible. In that heavenly home, each believer has an abiding place perfectly suited to them, where they belong.

95 ¶ We shall be made new

It was our helplessness—our inability to extract ourselves from sin and deception—that motivated God to rescue humanity, and not our intrinsic worth. And it is God alone who ascribes value to us. Not all humans are born equal, according to the world's values. There is great disparity of human worth: Some are born clever or beautiful, some are not; some are physically disabled; some people's ethnicity is despised by others; some suffer mental torment through self-hate or childhood trauma; some have to endure unkindness by people they cannot escape from. Life is unfair. Whilst God treasures all people who turn to Him, many believers are disadvantaged, in human terms. When such people find themselves loved by God their spirit awakens and they experience supernatural joy, but often their earthly condition remains the same; bodies are not always miraculously healed, people around them may continue to be cruel, tormented thoughts still break in to their consciousness. This is some believers' everyday reality. These kinds of injustices are seldom remedied in this life, even for followers of Christ: 'If for this life only we have hoped in Christ, we are of all men most to be pitied' (1 Corinthians 15:19).

God encourages each child He receives to surrender to Him their ego (the fleshly, natural 'man'), which is the part of us that engages with the twisted system of this world. He wants us to concentrate on our spiritual reality rather than the world's fallen values. Paul desired that the believers at Ephesus would have revelation of their spiritual identity: 'I pray that the eyes of your heart will be enlightened so you will know the hope to which He has called you, the riches of His glorious inheritance in the saints, and the surpassing greatness of His power for us who believe' (Ephesians 1:18-19).

When our body finally dies, all our struggles and disadvantages end; every inequality of human worth will drop away in eternity—when all is remade. In JRR Tolkien's book, *The Return of the King*, one of the characters, amazed to discover his dear friend is alive, asks: 'Is everything sad going to come untrue?'. If we apply that same question to believers' lives, the answer is 'yes', for there will be no sorrow in eternity. When John was given visions of heaven, he heard a loud voice from the throne of God, proclaiming that, 'God Himself will dwell with His people and be their God. He will wipe every tear from their eyes and there will be no more death or mourning or crying or pain, for the former things have passed away.' Then the One seated on the throne said, 'I am making everything new!' (see Revelation 21:3-5). In heaven our bodies will not be subject to sickness, torment or disability, but we shall be like the risen Lord Jesus: 'Our citizenship is in heaven, and it is from there that we eagerly await a Saviour, the Lord Jesus Christ, who will transform our lowly bodies into the likeness of His glorious body' (Philippians 3:20-21). Our future imperishable body may be difficult to imagine, but this is God's promise to those He loves.

96 ¶ We embody God's ultimate plans

Father God has a grand plan to redeem humanity and the earth: 'For the creation waits with eager longing for the revealing of the children of God; for the creation was subjected to futility, not of its own will but by the will of the one who subjected it, in hope that the creation itself will be set free from its bondage to decay and will obtain the freedom of the glory of the children of God. We know that the whole creation (Greek: ktisis) has been groaning in labor pains until now' (Romans 8:19-22 NRSV). After Jesus had risen from the dead He commissioned His followers to 'Go into all the world and preach the gospel to all creation (Greek: ktisis)' (Mark 16:15). Here the same Greek word is used, indicating that human beings are part of the creation that is suffering from futility, which is the absence of purpose. Therefore in the above sense, God's salvation has a wider cosmic dimension, and God's children are the forerunners of His ultimate plans for restoration.

It was the fall of humanity that brought about the bondage of decay that is now inflicted on creation—against its own will, since creation never chose to capitulate to the devil. Adam and Eve were meant to be faithful stewards of the earth, but they failed. And because God has restored believers, these are intended to be faithful stewards of the earth today: 'Think of us in this way, as servants of Christ and stewards of God's mysteries. Moreover, it is required of stewards that they be found trustworthy' (1 Corinthians 4:1-2). Stewards are responsible for whatever is entrusted to them, so believers are encouraged to seek God's revelation to find solutions to the seemingly intractable problems and injustices of this world, and to fully expect Him to provide us with the necessary wisdom: 'If any of you lacks wisdom, let him ask God, who gives to everyone generously and ungrudgingly, and it will be given to him' (James 1:5).

When human beings tried to create their own glory by attempting to build the tower of Babel as high as the heavens, God disciplined them by confusing their language, and limiting their capabilities (see Genesis 11:4-8). In Christ, the effects of this discipline are reversed, and believers can discover their full potential to create and instigate restoration. Consequently, whenever believers are 'in the Spirit' their group activities are trustworthy, because they will not harm themselves, other people, or the planet.

Shortly before Christ was crucified He petitioned the Father to give believers awareness of their unity through the glory He imparts: 'I have given them the glory that you gave Me, that they may be one as We are one' (John 17:22). And as we see in the above passage from Romans, it is the glory Christ has given the children of God that will ultimately liberate creation itself. Believers are part of the spiritual union between the Trinity, humanity and the rest of creation, and the

Father desires us to live in mindfulness of this reality. We shall only experience true unity once we recognise the glory of God in every believer. Jesus chose 'all the wrong people', overriding the system of religious superiority that dominated the time and place of His incarnation. Today, He continues to seek out these 'wrong kinds' of people, and He still gives them His glory. Whenever we remain blind to the glory within other believers, as well as those who will come to believe in the future, seeing them only in natural human terms, we shall miss the unity that God desires, which brings inherent blessing (see Psalm 133).

It is understood that when we are in Paradise with Christ there will be no disunity. But, here and now, when believers experience true spiritual unity they are more likely to discover their own redeemed identity, because their interaction awakens an awareness of being children of God. Just as the book of Proverbs states, 'As iron sharpens iron, so one person sharpens another' (Proverbs 27:17), believers spark in one another further revelation and appreciation of the ways of God, at the same time sensing the real presence of Jesus: 'Where two or three are gathered together in My name, I am there in their midst' (Matthew 18:20). All creation waits for the children of God to be revealed.

CONCLUDING REMARKS

Now that you have read our presentation of the gospel we would like to reiterate a couple of points.

Firstly, all believers are on a journey with God, and our understanding of His ways increases as we go through life. Therefore, we do not assume that everything we have written in this book will be our final understanding of these things. Similarly, we urge you not to take what we have written at face value, but you can bring your thoughts and reactions before your heavenly Father because, as Jesus said, 'the Father Himself loves you' (John 16:27). Believers benefit from dialoguing together, discussing the things of God. But having listened and considered, we need to go to Father God and ask Him what He has to say. He is our ultimate 'dialogue partner', and He is always pleased to give us new insights into His ways: 'Trust in the Lord with all your heart and do not lean on your own understanding;

in all your ways concede to Him, and He will make your paths straight' (Proverbs 3:5-6). If we remain in close relationship with God, submitting our views and opinions to Him, then asking what He has to say, we are less likely to lose our first love and excitement.

Secondly, Jesus made an appeal to His disciples: 'Do not call anyone on earth 'father,' for you have one Father, and He is in heaven' (Matthew 23:9). He further explains that in order to be a disciple, a person will prioritise God's wishes above all human demands: 'Anyone who loves their father or mother more than Me is not worthy of Me; anyone who loves their son or daughter more than Me is not worthy of Me' (Matthew 10:37). It is crucial that believers know their heavenly Father and trust His goodness, the way Jesus did, because when we know the Father's love we become confident of our intrinsic worth. However, believers' spiritual growth will be hindered if they seek to gain kudos through association with people they revere as spiritual heroes. This is not a new phenomenon, Paul encountered the same tendency in believers of his day: Clearly you still have not grown in your faith, because there is rivalry and factions among you. You are behaving like the world when one of you says, 'I'm following Paul,' and another says, 'I'm following Apollos.' Who on earth do you think Apollos is? And who on earth is Paul? Although you came to believe through us, remember we are merely servants of God, doing what He tells us (see 1 Corinthians 3:3-9). Paul teaches it is unspiritual to elevate human personalities, and advises believers to emulate his own practice of imitating Christ: 'Be imitators of me, just as I also imitate Christ' (1 Corinthians 11:1), and of course, Christ's earthly life perfectly demonstrates the leading of the Holy Spirit, and the fathering of God.

Janet Lock and Simon Mouatt

ABOUT THE BOOK
NAILED—RECLAIMING THE GOSPEL

"*Nailed—Reclaiming the Gospel* is a collection of statements about the three persons of the Trinity, and how they relate to humanity. The bible encourages believers to 'proclaim the goodness of the One who brought us out of darkness into His glorious light'. The authors have endeavoured to restate the fact that God is loving and kind, despite theological intimations to the contrary. Our book challenges the reader to take a fresh look at the good news that Jesus brought, in person, to the world—which amounts to the fact that there is a Father who loves us consistently, who wants the best for us and who has the power to rescue us from our mess".

"…powerful writers that will make Jesus Christ come alive for the readers. This book is relevant and timely".
Dimas Salaberrios, Author of 'Street God', New York.

"The book is a good presentation and overview of the Christian faith and the gospel, and its significance. It is also very structured, which corresponds to German thinking!".
Micha Siebeneich, Pastor, Treffpunkt Leben, Germany